Wonderful
Xinjiang

王 蒙 和 他 的 新 疆

CULTURAL CHINA—MAN AND THE LAND

Wonderful
Xinjiang

王 蒙 和 他 的 新 疆

A Photographic Journey of China's Largest Province

As told through the pen of Wang Meng

Reader's
Digest

The Reader's Digest Association, Inc.
Pleasantville, New York / Montreal / Hong Kong

Project Editors: Susan Randol, Longgen Chen
Project Designers: Yiping Yang, Naiqing Xu, Zongpei Jia
Interior and Cover Design: Yinchang Yuan
Interior and Cover Design Consultant: Nick Anderson
Senior Designer: George McKeon
Executive Editors: Ying Wu, Dolores York
Associate Publisher, Trade Publishing: Christopher T. Reggio
President & Publisher, Trade Publishing: Harold Clarke

Text by Wang Meng
Photographs by Alkin Khadir
Translation by Yaw-Tsong Lee

Library of Congress Cataloging in Publication Data
Wang, Meng.
    Wonderful xinjiang: a photographic journey through the pen of Wang Meng.
        p. cm.
    Includes index.
    ISBN 0-7621-0639-5
    1. Xinjiang Uygur Zizhiqu (China)–Description and travel. I. Title.

    DS793.S62W245 2004
    915.1'6046–dc22

Address any comments about *Wonderful Xinjiang* to:
    The Reader's Digest Association, Inc.
    Adult Trade Publishing
    Reader's Digest Road
    Pleasantville, NY 10570-7000

rd.com For more Reader's Digest products and information, visit our website.

Printed in China

1 3 5 7 9 10 8 6 4 2

On My Way to Xinjiang

I
At the Jiayu Pass the wind wolves howl,
Where does the sky begin and the desert end?
Frontier mountains far from the capital
With a smile urge me on to their land.

II
Through many suns and moons and time zones,
Hot and cold climes 'cross a thousand rivers,
I reunite with the snow of Tianshan
Whose soaring peaks haunted my dreams.

III
To hell and back my blood hasn't chilled,
Winds and rains my will have strengthened.
Sing I shall till my voice is stilled,
And give my all to this frontier land.

—Classical poems

Contents

Introduction

Forty years ago, with my life thrown into great turmoil, I resolutely pulled up stakes and moved my family westward to Xinjiang. I was filled with the noblest of intentions and even a romantic passion as I made the decision.

■ And Xinjiang did not let me down! It was so beautiful and so different, with its snowcapped mountains, glaciers, vast deserts, cyclones, oases, karez wells, seasonal rivers, long meandering highways, intraregional air routes, vast strip farm fields, as well as white poplar trees, red willows, roses, melon patches, beets, and clovers. And then there were its steppes, dragon spruce forests, flocks of sheep, horses, cattle, and Kazak yurts.... I was awe-struck by its grand scale and magnificence and impressed by the Uygur language, oral and written, body movements, attire, interior décor, culinary customs, singing and dancing, musical instruments, religion, and culture. What a fascinating and unique wonder in the panorama of the multiethnic culture of China!

■ I am eternally indebted to Xinjiang. Xinjiang is forever etched in my heart and mind. It was she who gave me happiness and comfort in my most difficult moments, provided for me when I was in the most need, fortified me when I was most vulnerable, and cheered me up and supported me when I was in the deepest depression.

■ "Xinjiang is a wonderful place." This song should continue to be sung a hundred, nay, a thousand years hence. I am a witness to this wonder. I want to sing its praises. Xinjiang has been my El Dorado, even when I've been in the dumps. Xinjiang has been family to me, even as human relationships were subjected to all kinds of distortion. Xinjiang is one of the most attractive places in the world, even though there's room for further development. Xinjiang is a hauntingly beautiful song, a most splendid scroll painting that does not cease to unfold; it is a place filled with passion and expectation, dreams and untamed spirits, innocence and vitality.

—Wang Meng

王蒙和他的新疆

CHAPTER 1 | Xinjiang, My Second Home

Coming Home to Xinjiang

Samovar in the mud hut
And goat milk in the yurt,
Blooming roses and lacemaking
Under the grape trellises,
A hot spring gurgles
Out of rocky crannies.
Shedding the dust and fatigue
Of my travel from the capital,
I am now freshly vested
With the vigor of the Kunlun.
No sooner have we greeted
Than 'tis time to bid adieu,
A joyous shake of hands briefly
And already we part in sorrow.

Have I changed at all?
What happened hasn't happened,
I am yours still.
I've kept my Uygur sharpened,
Mattock on shoulder I travel,
To Dahuang Ditch heartened.

The names of those who are gone
In a vast starry sky shine.
The young ones have grown
Into rows of towering trees.
Cry, cry, in tears we choke,
With good earth under our heel.
Bygones are a puff of smoke
But friendship is solid as steel.

· · · · · · · · · · Let nature work its thousand wonders, for man lives no more than a hundred years.

—From recent writings

. . . . Even at a distance where sharp vision begins to fail, even in evening twilight, one can easily tell a sterile hill from a wooded one. The hills covered with trees would have soft contours and blue purplish hues. The sight assures you that delicate beauty awaits discovery in those mountains. At higher altitudes, the ever regal and haughty snow reigns. Unlike the first snow of early winter by the roadside, this glistening white snow is perennial. Who knows the vintage of the glacial silver crown and what ancient century it dates back to? The peaks in the distance topped by this beautiful tiara appear so phantasmagoric they sometimes appear more like a shimmering patch of purple gray clouds….

—From the novel *Valley of Eagles*

On the highway, occasional trucks laden with goods lumbered by, with the orange setting sun tracing an increasingly clear and palpable trajectory on their windshields. On a dirt road elsewhere in the timber belt, boys with their peaked caps worn sideways herded homeward the milk cows left in their care by commune members who owned the animals. As they sensed the proximity of "home," the cows started to moo with abandon, swaying their bellies and fat backsides in a lumbering but enthusiastic manner, raising swirls of dust about them.

—From the novel *Song God*

········Antiquity possesses a solemnity and a dignity that compel you to bow your haughty forehead.

—Recent writing

. . . . Hutubi bristles with launch pads that stand magnificently against the sky. The town of Manas takes its name from a hero of Kirghiz epics. The forest belt in the Shihezi area rings with songs celebrating the virtues of troops farming and garrisoning the border areas. The guideposts pointing respectively to the oil town of Dushanzi and to Kuytun, headquarters of the 7th Agricultural Division of the Garrison Corps, give an idea of the vastness of Xinjiang and broaden one's outlook. Jinghe is famous both for its successful desert reclamation and for its watermelons….

—From the article "On the Highway"

· · · · · · · · · · · · · · · · After an absence of fifteen years, I am back again! We've both come a long way. You look all right, Kashgar! I am fine too. You've never left my thoughts. As they say: I've hiked through the green mountains and I feel as young as ever. This time around I had the good fortune of visiting the outlying border town of Tashkorgan in the remote region of Kashgar, touring the border crossing of Hongqilafu, being received in the home of Tajik herdsmen, attending an eagle flute performance and taking a morning stroll in Tashkorgan under a light snow....

—From the article "Eternal Beauty"

· · · · · · · · The setting sun sprinkled a coat of gold dust on the crowns of the gracefully swaying poplar trees lining both sides of the road; the glitter then filtered down through the intertwined branches and foliage to settle softly on the surface of the gurgling water in the irrigation channel that had been flooded in anticipation of the planting of the winter wheat; this brightened up the water, making its flow seem cheerier. In the lush autumn grass by the road and alongside the ditch, goats and donkeys could be seen to occasionally pop up their heads, looking elegant and regal, thanks to a life of leisure and plenty.

—From the novel *Song God*

··················· The most interesting part of the day's itinerary was the campsite where we put up for the night. It was a small clearing called Wutai, ringed by mountains, a facility that sprang up to cater to the needs of travelers. It would begin to bustle at nightfall, with people eating sautéed mutton and washing it down with wine, travelers looking around for a bed or busy repairing radiators and clutches. Every morning before dawn the motors and engines of the cars and trucks would start up in chorus; and by daybreak the place would already be deserted....

—From the novel *Leisurely Travels*

O youthful years that are no more! In those days, every breeze felt like a caress, every drop of water soothed, every scudding cloud evoked reveries and every mountain gave you strength. When in youth, every song brought tears, the sight of every red banner quickened your pulse, every bugle call beckoned, and every fellow human being was adorable. Every moment, every day, you had the sense of carousing in a jubilant festival.

—From the novel *Bedraggled Horse*

Tashkorgan I

You are a mystery, Pamirs,
Untouchable, inscrutable
And inaccessible. I can only
Write a film script at your feet.

Rocks forming in calm and seclusion,
Rarefied air starved of oxygen,
Distant, soaring and snowbound mountains
Ringing the mighty Muztag Peak
As well as the many tongues you speak
Please stay unspoiled because we care.

Note: Some thirty years ago, the movie *Visitors from the Ice Mountain*
reinforced the fascination that Xinjiang and Tashkorgan held for me.
During my years in Xinjiang, however, I never got a chance to see
Tashkorgan. My long-cherished wish to visit it was finally granted in
October 1990, and I composed this poem to commemorate the occasion.
Muztag means "ice mountain." Tashkorgan is an autonomous Tajik
county. Tajik belongs to the Iranian branch of the Indo-European family
of languages.

· · · · · · · · · · · · · · · · · · Dark clouds already obscured a quarter of the sky, rendering the grass directly under them somber, broody, and a little eerie. One part of the scenery appeared as though seen through dark sunglasses and the remainder seen with the naked eye. The part of the grassland still bathed in sunlight was no longer green but had turned golden and was shrinking with the advance of the dark brown part.

—From the novel *Bedraggled Horse*

· · · · · · · · · · · · · · The military highway from Kashgar to Tashkorgan has left a particularly indelible impression on me. The road hugs the contour of the mountainside, with gigantic rocks cantilevered overhead. It was gouged from the midriff of the mountain with dynamite, which had failed to shear off the top, leaving the massive rocks hanging precariously over the road like the sword of Damocles; the sheer cliffs dropping off steeply from the road and the hairpin turns add piquancy to the traveler's sense of adventure and derring-do. Life is full of challenges, the road is fraught with dangers, and the driving is a daunting feat. Let's not harbor naive illusions of smooth motoring.

—From the article "On the Highway"

· · · · · · · · · · · · · · · · · · After that I came to the banks of the Ili River, to its torrential water that rushed on day and night. Heaven and earth became one as bonfires were lit. The rising sun sprinkled a shower of golden sequins on the surface of the turbid water carrying driftwood and fallen leaves downstream. Whitecaps played hide and seek; in the middle of the river were islets overgrown with a motley mix of wild shrubs. Occasionally chunks of earth could be heard to crash into the water with a roar as they separated from the riverbank. Eagles hovered overhead and wild ducks spreading their fawn-colored wings skimmed the water surface in a gliding motion. Lush grass carpeted the riverbanks, and from across the river, faint sounds of human and animal origin blew over from Chabuchaer…. All this conveyed a powerful sense of a dual quality of ruggedness and tenderness, happiness and sorrow, that intoxicated me and gave rise to an urge to sing, to versify. But despite the lightning and thunderclaps, and search as I may the sky and the earth, I could not produce the words that would remotely do justice to the celebration of the motherland, of Mother Earth, of this frontier land, and of its Ili River that is at once untamed and yet so closely bound up with the people.

O Ili River! Won't you allow me to sing your praises? Pray tell me how.

—From the novel *Leisurely Travels*

· · · · · · · · · Human eyes have yet to settle on this lake whose deep blue water is placid but pregnant with a certain angst. It is surrounded on three sides by magnificent peaks that remain snow-capped even in summer. The mountains are reflected in the smooth blue mirror of the lake. You often have a hard time telling whether the sky or the lake is bluer, and whether it's the snow-capped mountains in the distance or the mountains in the water that are more real and pure. In the end you are no longer sure if this mountain lake hundreds of miles in circumference is a mirage, a legend, or a fairy tale.

—From the novel *Leisurely Travels*

· · · · · · · · · Where have we met before? Is it in traditional Chinese landscape paintings? This scene reminds one of famous paintings such as "The Gentleman," "The Mountain Trail," "The Gushing Spring," and "Listening to the Pine." Or have we met in Andersen's mysterious tale of *The Ice Maiden*? Or maybe in well-loved poems from the Tang dynasty? "Somewhere in the mountain I reckon, high above the dense clouds hidden"; "not a calendar in the mountain, I forget the year after the cold season"; "through the pines moonlight filters, o'er the rocks the clear spring gurgles"; "penetrating the dense forest, dying sunlight revisits the moss."

—From the novel *Valley of Eagles*

Ili is first of all the name of a river. Swelled by the waters of the Kunges, the Tekes, and the Hashi rivers, the Ili meanders westward through cascading rapids and numerous bends, carrying sand and silt with it, to finally pour into the Balkhash Lake in the Soviet Union.

My first visit to the Ili River was in the spring of 1965. Before reaching the riverbank, I had to pass through an expanse of waterlogged marshland covered with the mysterious violet blooms of the Indian aster (*Kalimeris indica*). The tents near the top of a slope indicated that the Kazak herdsmen of the pastoral regiment were grazing their animals in this region. We came upon a section of dunes and bluffs, probably carved out of the riverbank by flood water during high-water periods. The tottering masses of earth of varying heights stood like ruins on ancient battlefields, imparting a sense of power and portending danger and destruction. They bespoke patience and strength and exuded an eerie and epic beauty.

—From the novel *Leisurely Travels*

Note: The Balkhash Lake is located in present-day Kazakhstan.

· · · · · · · · · W hen it snows in Ili City, at the foot of the Tianshan Mountains, be sure to observe the sky, the mountains, the fields, the trees, and the courtyards. Look at people's eyebrows, beards, faces, turbans, and dresses; pay attention to the manes of horses and the tops of all kinds of vehicles. You will be rewarded with great excitement and contentment in this exercise. You will find that this authentically northern snow is testimony to the grandness of the universe, a gift from heaven, a silent but jubilant dance. It signifies a genuine equality and brotherly love. This snow of the north country symbolizes an eternal fortitude combined with a genuine belief in the virtue of taking things as they come.

—From the novel *Leisurely Travels*

The whole sky glowed with the sun still low on the horizon. Against the backdrop of the clear, light blue sky, clouds tinted red, yellow, and black stretched, like a long fluffy strand of silk, for as far as the eyes could see. The tall mountain peaks truncating the strand of clouds at the two ends also seemed to double as pillars supporting the clouds. The "forest" of mountains near and far was still an amalgam of dark masses. The one that appeared closest and seemingly almost within reach loomed like a cactus plant with a pointed (or was it blunted?) peak silhouetted against the sky. Its two sides were cliffs that dropped off steeply while front to back it formed a thin slab, much like the tablet held by officials in attendance on a Chinese emperor. In the back light, the trees on the mountain bristled like spines on a cactus plant.

—From the novel *Valley of Eagles*

· · · · · · · · · · · · · · · · Along the way one is greeted by countless peaks covered by new snow, sheer cliffs of rock, densely wooded mountains that loom like cactus plants, small bridges made of stone, of wood, or of concrete, tall silhouettes of spruce trees in groups of varying density displaying myriad gestures, and wooden gratings built on the slopes bordering the road to snag snow avalanches, as well as eagles, crows, and birds of unknown names flying at different altitudes.

—From the novel *Valley of Eagles*

· · · · · · · · · · · · · · · · We are greeted by a wispy silvery cascade that drops down the cliff face to join the ebullient, galloping water in the mountain creek. Overhead a multi-leaved poplar tree (*Populus Euphratica*), with its dense foliage, stands a watchful guard over the mountain road. It is also like a hospitable host coming out a great distance to greet his visitors. It seems to herald the end of the forlorn Gobi and treeless mountains and the beginning of a verdant world of plenty. Underfoot is a dense mass of weeds of many vintages, a mixture of withered yellow and lush green. In the midst of the weeds stand a few crab apple trees whose gnarled and twisted branches struggle skyward. At the sight of their bumper crops of small, tart fruit, one's mouth immediately starts to water.

—From the novel *Bedraggled Horse*

．．．．．．．．．．．．．．．．．．．The summer pasture is so quiet, this night in the mountain valley. The near-full moon finally clears the mountaintop after a long, slow ascent, illuminating the valley and imparting a glitter to the water in the mountain creek, which shimmers, breaks up, and coalesces again. The scaly bark of the white birch trees glisten in the night, and their leaves rustle with love. Now the tops of the yurts are also bathed in moonlight. In the moonlight, the mountains look even more regal and somber. As a breeze rises, it sends ripples through the grass and the leaves. The water in the creek, the smoke issuing from homes, and even the stones in this wilderness start to quiver. A scattering of mooing and barking…and the valley settles back into deeper silence.

—From the novel *The Last Tao*

· · · · · · · · · As Cao Qianli looked down, the river current seemed to have become swifter, churning up spumes of water that played with the glare of the sunlight as if through a prism, causing him to feel a little dizzy. He had decided to tighten the reins and spur the belly of his mount to prod it to get out of this unsafe spot, when out of the corner of his eye, he caught sight of the snowcapped peaks in the distance. The snowy peaks displaying a bluish tint under the sun appeared to be amused by his flustered state.

—From the novel *Bedraggled Horse*

· · · · · · · · I had no idea I would be rewarded with such a breathtaking view when I looked down, as if from the window of an airplane! The valley was littered with rocks of all sizes, shaped variously like tigers, elephants, monkeys, birds, artillery shells, bottles, and drums. They looked as if they were reclining, standing, wrestling, or leaning against one another, embracing or separating or running from each other. Where had so many rocks come from? Had there been a shower of meteorites the night before?

—From the novel *Valley of Eagles*

· · · · · · · · · · · · · · · · · · The valley has come back to me, the valley with mountains on both sides of the road running parallel to a creek, bordered by grass and trees! You, meadow fescues and trefoils, you, fleaworts and burdocks, prince's feathers and knotweeds, dandelions and purslanes, wild mints and onions as well as mountain grapes and strawberries, you are back! And you, Siberian crab apples and water willows, wild apple and mulberry trees, birches and poplars, cedars and mountain elms, you've all come back to me!

—From the novel *The Last Tao*

Lake Kanas

Don't say there's no fairyland,
I've found Shangri-la in Lake Kanas.
On turquoise waves she spreads her graceful arms,
Spruce trees and mists part to unveil her beauty.
Fireflies among weeds take leave of summer,
White clouds, first snows pine for lofty peaks.
Twin arcs of rainbow grace the fresh-washed sky,
Forgotten are man's meanness and time gone by!

Note: Shown in the photo are the author Wang Meng
and his wife, Fang Rui.

Tianshan Mountain Road in Snow

That world of snow and ice
Often comes back to me,
Mountain valley strewn with stones
Carcasses of cars gone off the road.
Better wrapped in iron chains
Our fast spinning tires.
Will rows of dragon spruces
And wooden grills built by shepherds
For their sheep flocks and you folks
Stop the advance of avalanches?

Ahead and in back of us, the road surface is densely pockmarked by the footprints of cows, horses, and sheep, signifying the intimate, symbiotic coexistence of man and animal. Nature wakes up with replenished life and energy; the air is now refreshed and moistened. What particularly intrigues and charms someone who has traveled over an hour through the desert is the dark brown soil that seems to ooze moisture and the shrubs that break out of the earth and tightly grip the soil to protect it against the erosion of floodwater. This is an Eden in the mountains! This is a land of milk and honey in the northwest frontier land! This is an ideal human habitat if ever there was one!

—From the novel *Bedraggled Horse*

· · · · · · · · · The highway was built for much of the way parallel to a mountain creek that comes into view now on one's right, now on one's left, sometimes ahead and sometimes to the rear, alternating between bright spots and shadowy stretches but never too far from the road. We can see the water flowing briskly in the creek, leaping, sending up sprays, turning, cascading, and pausing before resuming its irresistible advance. The music of the gurgling water is a thousand times more mellifluous than the din of car engines and screeching tires that numb one's nerves and ears.

—From the novel *Valley of Eagles*

· · · · · · · · · · · · · · · · · As dawn chases off darkness, the mountain masses turn incrementally greener. The peaks on the horizon present all manner of strange shapes, resembling a hat, a sword, a cane, or a bergamot orange. Some appear to have been cleaved with a knife, to have split down the middle, or to piggyback on others. As the vista broadens ahead of us, we can see gently rolling hills in the distance, whose white tops suggest an altitude that is much higher than our camping station.

—From the novel *Valley of Eagles*

. . . . T his water originates from the mountain creek flowing by the little wood shack, the very creek that has so captivated me and that I adore so much! We have been trying to catch up with the crystal water that flowed by the wooden hut this morning; with the car having the upper hand in speed, by nightfall we will have caught up with the water that received the reflection of the cactus-shaped peaks.

—From the novel *Valley of Eagles*

· · · · · · · · · · Eternal Turpan, eternal Suleiman's Minaret, eternally aspiring to the heavens!

—From recent writings

王
蒙
和
他
的
新
疆

CHAPTER 2 | Folks and I

Do you know that this evening a bespectacled Bayandai-Pekinese man has come back to you from thousands of miles away to say hello and to open his heart to you?

■ Mama Heliqihan, are you coming down tonight to roam among the tall poplar trees? When you passed away on October 6, 1979, I was writing furiously in a small noisy guesthouse in Beijing, pouring out the joy of picking up my pen again after a long hiatus, unaware of your untimely death from illness. Pardon me, Apa, for not sending you off, for not being able to attend your funeral, your *naizier*. I drank milk tea prepared by you almost daily for six years. As water boiled in the enamel kettle, you sat by the stove, talking and laughing with me. After the boiled water was poured into the enamel pot, you scooped up a pinch of salt with your hand and put it in a ladle made from a whole gourd, passed the gourd through the water, and added in a bowl of precooked and condensed cow milk with milk skin floating on the surface. Finally, you ladled up some tea with the gourd, rinsed the milk bowl with it, and gave the gourd a last swirl in the pot. When the milk tea was done, the first bowl was always reserved for me. Sometimes you would say in your faltering Mandarin, "Lao Wang, dip!" On cue, I would start to shred a big *nang* [crusty pancake] or a small *nang* or a corn *nang* containing tiny golden pieces of pumpkin into the milk tea. I was at first unaccustomed to this way of eating shredded food dipped in milk, considering it fit only for kindergarten kids. It was you who patiently initiated me into this custom. When you saw that I'd finally learned the proper way of eating and that I did not waste a single crumb of *nang*, you broke into such a smile of satisfaction that I can still see it vividly now. But where are you now? Where are you? Amid the rustling and whispering leaves of the poplar trees, I listen in vain for Apa's voice calling out to her Lao Wang.

■ Daddy Abdul Rahman, we've met again at last. In those years, I told you the story of my life. I recall your long pensive silence that day after hearing me out. When you spoke again, you said to me with confidence, "Lao Wang, this will not go on forever. Imagine! How can a country still be a country if it banishes its poets? Heads of state, officials, and poets are indispensable ingredients of a country. Rest assured, Lao Wang, that such a policy would not last for long." You did not have any schooling, did not know how to write your own name, did not know the Han language, and had not read any books, but you were unshaken in your belief. You expressed in your own language your belief that common sense, truth, and objective laws would eventually prevail against any one individual's will. Your belief has now been vindicated: Poets and writers have regained respectability in our country. Gone are the days when poets were rejected and ostracized! In the meantime, you have aged considerably.

■ I also remember Hasim Yusuf, then branch party secretary of the Second Brigade. On the eve of leaving Bayandai for Urumqi in 1971 to "await disposition by the Party," I was told by Comrade Hasim, "Don't worry. Go with peace of mind! If they [meaning the powers that be in Urumqi] do not need you, we need you. If they do not understand you, we understand you. You are welcome to come back at any time with your family. I'll have the necessary residence papers ready for you. If you need housing, we will allot you a piece of land and build the foundation for you. We will solve all your difficulties." What loyalty and friendship! Folks of Bayandai! I received so much support and encouragement from you in my darkest hours. An old adage says aptly, "It is enough to have one real friend." In Bayandai, hundreds of poor and lower-middle peasants were my real friends, and in my most difficult and chaotic days, I did not lose my faith or optimism, my joie de vivre, or my will to live. People still marvel at the absence of any white hair on my head and my robust health at the ripe age of forty-seven. I actually had very poor health in my youth. Why have I been blessed with better health and greater vigor in the aftermath of my trials and tribulations? It's all thanks to you, all of you—Abdul Rahman, Izhaq, Hasim Yusuf, Abdul Karim, Jin Guozhu, Amdullah, Mansur Esan…. Your support and help, your empathy, and your brotherly love have warmed my heart and given me courage. When I came to the village of the Fourth Brigade and visited Daddy Izhaq, he couldn't stop crying. Our hearts went out to each other; we felt for one another. What more could I ask for?

························As I stroll leisurely on the poplar-lined country lane, every tree, every house, every wooden door, every spiral of smoke rising out of *nang* [crusty pancake] baking ovens, every dog bark and rooster cry evoke fond memories. Yes, I used to draw water from this clear irrigation channel! To draw water, all that the impoverished Apa possessed was a gnarled pole with two odd-sized buckets. It was not much of a pole, because it was not even flat and would not stay put on one's shoulder but threatened to slide off at any moment.

—From the article "Homecoming"

· · · · · · · · · · · · · · · · · ·From 1965 to 1971, I lived in this Uygur peasant house in Ili, situated on the old Urumqi-Ili Highway. Heavy traffic created a constant cloud of dust in the environs. Of course, my landlord Daddy Mumin, and his wife, Mama Ayimhan, were at that time already using that rusty lock on their door. But good traditions die hard; the lock threaded through the last link of the iron chain on our wooden door often remained unbolted. The lock was more symbolic than realistic. Sometimes there wasn't even a symbolic lock when only a small piece of wood or a rigid grass stem was inserted into the chain link. Symbolism then gave way to surrealism and metaphysical symbolic logic.

—From the novel *The Mud Hut with Its Door Left Ajar*

· · · · · · · · · · · · · · · · One's hometown and childhood are wondrous things. When Old Daddy talked about the south country with Khasim, tears glittered in his eyes. This is the inextinguishable afterglow of hometown and childhood.

—From the novel *The Mud Hut with Its Door Left Ajar*

· · · · · · · · Aydanak, what a sweet-sounding name! It means "white as moonlight." Whiteness, in our language, symbolizes beauty, purity, and goodness. Kazaks are very good at inventing all kinds of names. Although I stayed with Uncle for only one summer, this young girl tending cattle by the Ili River already came to my attention. She had dense, long, black hair and a round, rosy cherubic face that framed a pair of eyes sparkling with innocence and life occasionally tinged with wistfulness.

—From the novel *Song God*

I've met his present wife. She is called Mawolitam and is in her twenties. She has lively fierce-looking eyes, and enjoys walking barefoot in the street, her calves caked with mud and her mouth busily cracking dried sunflower seeds, keeping the husks inside to be spat out after some accumulation. She has a booming voice with a shrill edge that reminds one of fabric being ripped.

—From the novel *Pale Gray Eyes*

····················Little Ismael is actually not small at all. He is also known as Pockmarked Ismael because, as the nickname suggests, his face is covered with pocks. But I've not seen a more handsome pockmarked man. When I first met him in 1965, he had just turned thirty. He sported a Kazak felt hat that resembled a catamaran and a dense black handlebar (Budenny-style) moustache that swept upward. He had big round eyes and generously sized nostrils that exhaled like bellows. Physically stalwart and never without a triumphant, smiling air on his face, he cuts an authoritative figure that disarms you instantly, convincing you that the pocks rather accent his virility and reinforce the image of a rugged individual.

—From the novel *Good Man Ismael*

NOTE: Semyon Mikhailovich Budenny (1883-1973) was a Russian military leader.

Though not very tall, Mahinur was of stocky build. Her fair facial complexion was tinged with a rosy blush and she had evenly proportioned features. She inherited her flat head, however, from her father. She liked to dress herself in light-colored shirts, dark-colored skirts, short socks, and white or blue sneakers. Her large feet accented her youth and energy. True to her spontaneous disposition, she often allowed her hair to escape from under her scarf and her skirt to expose part of her legs, a no-no in the countryside. This gave her an air of a city person or someone having received secondary education.

—From the novel *O Muhamed Ahmed!*

· · · · · · · · · · · · · · · · · They had big, dark, round eyes and thick, long, black eyelashes. Naturally they liked to eat figs, which left a lingering fruity sweetness and fragrance on their palms. Oh, it has been such a long time since I last heard those girls slapping the figs in their palms before eating the flattened fruit!

—From the novel *Valley of Eagles*

· · · · · · · · · · · · · · · · Turdi was one of the most handsome, modest and good-natured men around. His good nature was not, however, without a touch of bitterness. He was thirty-three, tall and broad-shouldered, handsome and urbane with his large eyes. Except for a complexion that was dark to a fault, he had first-class looks. But his bashfulness gave an impression of inadequate masculinity. Ali was friendly to him in a patronizing way and ordered him about unceremoniously. As for Turdi, he had a steeliness behind his gentle façade; he treated Ali, and probably others, with brotherly affection and deference without letting down his guard.

—From the novel *Valley of Eagles*

Daddy Mumin was venerated in the village for his probity, for being a civic-minded law-abiding citizen who observed scrupulously the teachings of Islam. He was consulted whenever there was to be a funeral, and he never begrudged any help he could offer. He would pitch in to wash the body before wrapping it in a white shroud, join in the prayers, the seventh-day memorial and even participate in the funeral procession. He would thus busy himself for several days on end with a grave sorrowful mien. "Oh us mortals!" was the only lamentation he occasionally uttered during these days of unusual silence. This was well before it became fashionable to make such pithy utterances about the human condition.

—From the novel *The Mud Hut with Its Door Left Ajar*

.................I saw his four children, who were almost of
equal height and all of whom attended the Han school. They had big bright eyes
and superior intelligence. When their mother called out to them, she prolonged
the pronunciation of their familiar names; for example, her youngest daughter
was called "Khalibinur," a name I used in one of my novels, meaning "glow in
one's heart," but her mother would call her familiarly "Khalibish," a sound
extremely pleasing to the ear.

—From the novel *Emila's Sentimental Journey*

· · · · · · · · · · · · · · · M y six-year-old brother had a world of his own, consisting of, among other things, bricks, stones, nails, bits of wood, mud, earth, cats, dogs, water, and fire. Already at the young age of six, he rolled up a dirty piece of paper, lit it before snuffing it out, and smoked it like a cigarette. He didn't generally bother Rayla but it was within his right to demand food and drink from her and ask her to mend his ripped trouser legs.

—From the novel *Splendors of a Frontier Town*

Nostalgia I

Looking for you
Darkly in the courtyard,
I softly mock and mourn,
Sorrow lost I know not when.

. . . . E specially after the return of Dawolat, the youngest son of Uncle Izhaq, he came home neatly and smartly dressed, wearing a serge peaked cap, a Dacron youth jacket, and denim riding breeches. No cow dung could be detected on his leather boots, no burrs on his trousers, and no dust on his shirt.

—From the novel *The Last Tao*

Nostalgia II

Then you got on in years,
And were no longer invited to
Weddings, circumcisions, and waltzes.
You were quickly forgotten
Like lightning in Ramadan,
Dignified tears of young goats and you,
And casts of wriggling earthworms.
Waves broke in droplets of sodium chloride,
To marinate the clouds. Clouds of dust
Bore down heavily on your dainty nose.

· · · · · · · Under the head-scarf are the equally remarkable eyebrows dyed dark green with "Osman" grass. These eyebrows tug at Cao Qianli's heartstrings. What heavenly beauty! Can the roaring waves not wash away the dark green of her eyebrows?

—From the novel *Bedraggled Horse*

········Ismael's wife was called Ma Xiuxian. Two long braids peeked out from under her purplish red scarf, framing an oval face. Long earrings dangled from her earlobes and copper bracelets adorned her wrists. She was fair complexioned and petite in build; she often nursed her baby while carrying on a conversation in a soft voice. The exterior of her good nature, soft-spokenness, and docility masked a steely resolve.

—From the novel *Good Man Ismael*

．．．．．．．．．Whom are they waving at?
Why are they so merry? How friendly they are!
You should hear their happy laughter.

—From recent writings

· · · · · · · · · · · · · · · · The ever-merry Kirim Khoja passed away. We paid a call to his wife at his home in Urumqi. The beautiful Guhalia with golden hair cried uncontrollably in my arms.

After that we stood in front of the hanging rug for a group photo. We mourned the absent friend who had left behind these objects impregnated with his memory.

—From recent writings

Impromptus

(Two poems)

I heard the water sing
Washing my feet in the ditch,
And drank tea under the bower
Lovely with hanging melons.
Young calves greeted guests
With proud moo moos
While baby swallows trilled
Affectionate coo coos.

When broad beans bloom
It's time to hoe the bitter bean.
With roses fresh faded
Indian asters grow thin.
Folks line up to praise
Seafarers sailing away,
Honing their scythes
For the summer harvest.

Beautiful Kazaks! Good-hearted Kazaks! Kazaks with their simple ways! Uncle Izhaq went to the length of butchering a sheep, cutting the meat into strips that he salted and hung out to cure, insisting that Halidam take it to Beijing and then to Australia. He didn't believe that mutton of such high quality could be found outside of the Tianshan valley; nor did he think that there was anything more delicious and worth eating than mutton. Could Halidam have refused?

—From the novel *Emila's Sentimental Journey*

· · · · · · · · · · · · · · · · · · One day after work, I saw Emila with a tall and handsome man who had beautiful large eyes and broad shoulders. Emila, who had been getting plumper, introduced her husband to me, her eyes crinkled into a smile. His name was Shamsudin, which means the sun in Arabic (or is it Persian?). Even an outsider like me could feel the warmth and glow of that sun.

—From the novel *Emila's Sentimental Journey*

· · · · · · · · · · · · · · · · "To hell with writers and with novels! I'm done with those things now! I am a peasant! A peasant of the Maolayuzi Commune! I work with a mattock. I drink milk tea and eat corn *nang* [crusty pancake]; I often share a drink or two with my Uygur friends," I said, winking like a Uygur. "What a happy life!" I cheered.

—From the novel *Emila's Sentimental Journey*

Friendship

No need to clink glasses
To cement friendship.
Nor need to proclaim it
To the whole wide world.
All friendship means is
We shall not forget.

· · · · · · · He has a house, a wife, and children. He has his domicile in Shang-a-watai on Lake Yuepu, but he is seldom home. He is always on the road, earning extra money with his numerous crafts, such as butchering, tanning, rug making, mat weaving, cobbling, and haircutting. He also knows something about Uygur traditional medicine and is able to make diagnoses and write prescriptions, claiming to be half a traditional doctor.

—From the novel *The Mud Hut with Its Door Left Ajar*

· O ne trait in Daddy Mumin's character is his aversion to giving people a heads-up about his future movements. When Mama asks Daddy about his plans for the next day, his stock answer is: "Who knows?" or "Let *Huda* [God] decide!"

—From the novel *The Mud Hut with Its Door Left Ajar*

. . . . I am still me! Hometown, childhood, Mother Earth, don't you recognize me? I am Halidam, your Kazak daughter, descendant of your herdsmen. Halidam who was born, raised, and grew up on horseback!

—From the novel *The Last Tao*

Tashkorgan II

Traveling great distances,
Racing scudding clouds,
Through thirty suns and moons,
Muddy roads, hairpin turns,
Highways soaring like songs.
Up icy peaks, down deep gorges,
With gigantic rocks hanging
Like the sword of Damocles…
I came to you at last.

Taking one deep breath
I am acclimatized.
At the first encounter
We pour out our hearts
And in an age-old ritual
Receive libations and toasts,
Inebriated with the limpidity
Of the lake of the heart.

· · · · · · · · · · · · · · · As fate would have it, I ended up living in this small residential compound for two whole years. I witnessed many unimportant but unforgettable incidents, unforgettable scenes, unforgettable human interactions, and unforgettable circumstances and objects that were beyond the imagination of people living in big cities or intellectuals or government officials.

—From the novel *Leisurely Travels*

Tall Cathay poplar tree, are you the sapling we planted in 1968? You were then puny, scraggly, and almost leafless. Cows, goats, donkeys, and horses as well as passing carts and wheels constantly put your survival to the test. Now you are a strapping adult. You and your contemporaries in tight formation survey from your dizzying height the roads and planting fields around you and the Lilliputian humans who once protected and nurtured you and are still tending you. Do you know the old forest ranger who ran things then? And who will be your dynamic new managers? Do you know that tonight a bespectacled Bayandai-Pekinese man has traveled thousands of miles to come back to you, to say hello and confide in you?

—From the article "Homecoming"

· · · · · · · · · · · · · · · · Life on the eternally verdant summer pasture of the Kazaks has not changed down through the ages. In the way of the ancients, the teakettle was put on the stove, the table napkin was spread, and the loaves of *nang* [crusty pancake] were laid out, with the top ones broken as invitation to the guests to partake. The hoary-haired Kazak auntie sat in front of the milk tea she was preparing in the tradition of her ancestors, as tears trickled down her cheeks in her feeling of loss at the imminent departure of Halidam for a distant land, mixed with the joy at yet another opportunity in her life to be with Halidam.

—From the novel *The Last Tao*

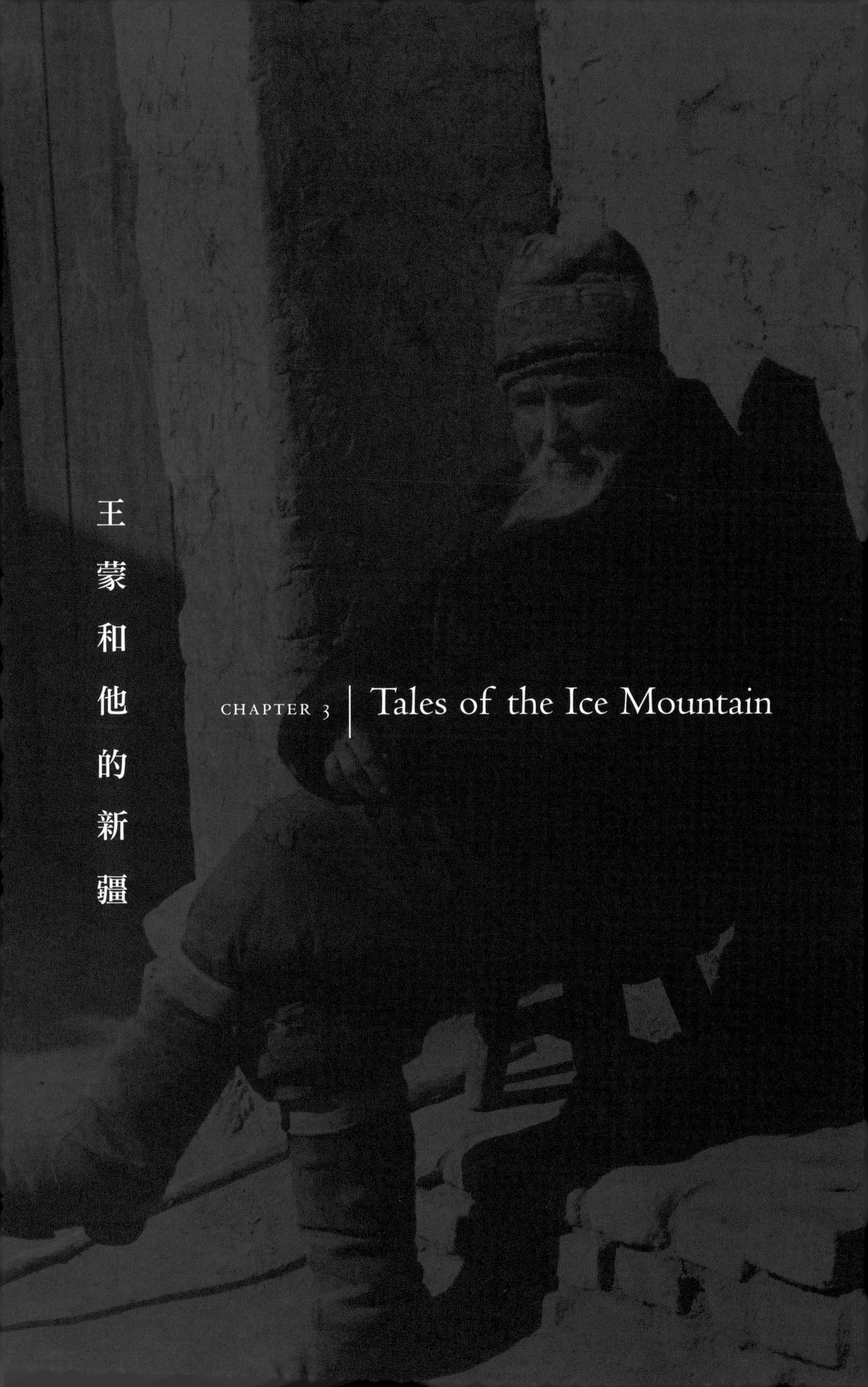

王
蒙
和
他
的
新
疆

CHAPTER 3 | Tales of the Ice Mountain

I wonder if you still remember that winter day deep in the mountains covered by the first snow, how the open-top truck carrying you and your companions hurtled toward the heart of the logging region on the meandering mountain road that was shaped like a long silk ribbon thrown up in the air by a dancer. Do you remember? The wind nearly blew off your hat, and an eagle with its wings spread out hovered at an angle above the front of the truck, its eyes striking you as sad.

■ Do you remember the gorge deep in the mountain range littered with boulders that looked as if they might have been left by a meteorite shower the night before? And the mountain stream with its singing water, rushing forth in its playful way, now sending aloft sprays of water like pearls and snowflakes, now swirling in intricate woven patterns? And how above the stream there hovered a never-dissipating mist, the mountain road, and occasional golden rays of sunlight?

■ Do you remember the aroma of the spruce trees, the animal footprints on the thin layer of timidly thawing snow, and the loggers' lilting, resonant, and awe-inspiring work songs? Remember the stubbornness, the joyous disposition and pride of those men with superior brawn in their arms? And the drivers waiting for their trucks to be loaded, anxious as ants trapped in a hot pan, but unable to do otherwise than grin and bear it?

■ And the little log cabin in the woods, bonfires in the night, Kazak herdsmen's pelt coats and hats, the buzzing of the power saws, and the roar of big branches splitting off the tree trunks?

■ And the desert and Gobi stretching to the horizon, the alarms in the middle of the night announcing emergencies and crises, the steaming bowl of noodles garnished with shreds of ginger and scallions, and the whole house erupting into laughter, breaking the quiet isolation?

Like local Uygur girls, she wore earrings that shone like gold and ruby without being made of precious metal or stone. She also had a sheer nylon scarf embroidered with satiny silk, but she did not follow the local women's custom of wrapping it around their heads all year round but wore it mostly about her neck. When the wind became gusty, she would pull the scarf up to cover her head but would always leave more hair exposed than local women dared. She started this year to apply some light inconspicuous makeup, which in no way prevented her natural youthful complexion from coming through in all its glory. Of late she took to wearing a brown nylon (synthetic silk) jacket. She would occasionally put on a skirt, but most of the time she wore gray wool-blend pants. Her well-fitting clothes accented her good figure. Interestingly enough, she neither deliberately flattened her chest with tight girdles as local women did nor followed the fad of throwing out one's breasts among Uygur women in the capital of the Autonomous Region. She had moderate bodily curves that seemed just right without being conspicuous. In the matter of footwear, she adhered to the ancient local tradition of wearing knee-length leather boots on formal occasions, regardless of the season. At home she preferred walking about barefoot on the rugs.

—From the novel *Light of the Heart*

One unforgettable scene from my life in Ili: As I looked out of my window onto the street, toward the alley off to one side, I often saw these two Uygur girls talking under a poplar tree by a ditch in front of a small wooden door. One of them was dark-complexioned and stoutly built, her hair held by a crescent-shaped comb and a sky blue scarf perfunctorily covering the back of her head, leaving the tip of her thick braid exposed. She had two gold teeth. As she talked, her mouth would pucker into a pout, giving the impression that she was being coquettish or cross with someone. Her face was very expressive, and judging by the rapid opening and closing of her mouth, one sensed that she was a fast and loquacious talker bursting with a million things to say. The other girl, often with her back toward me, was tall and slim, with thin, curly hair. She kept nodding her head, and as she did so, I could sometimes glimpse her fluttering eyelashes.

—From the novel *Leisurely Travels*

· · · · · · · · Most of the girls here have a dark complexion tinged with a rosy tone and pretty eyes under bushy eyebrows. They look like phoenixes sprung out of a smelting furnace. They have a weakness for gold teeth, like to wear a red rose in their hair, dye their eyebrows dark green, and apply red polish on their fingernails, the palms of their hands, and soles of their feet.

—From the novel *Valley of Eagles*

$\cdot$ $\cdot$ $\cdot$ $\cdot$ $\cdot$ $\cdot$ $\cdot$ $\cdot$ $\cdot$ $\cdot$ $\cdot$ $\cdot$ $\cdot$ $\cdot$ $\cdot$ $\cdot$ Turahan always has a clean white scarf wrapped around her head. She likes to wear a white one-piece dress and a light gray blouse over it. Covering her feet and legs are a pair of cotton stockings blanched from repeated washings and calf-length leather boots with a wrinkled look from lack of brushing and polishing. In winter, spring, and autumn, rain or shine, she always wears overshoes that look brand new and well cleaned and brushed, unlike the mud- and dust-covered ones worn by most others.

—From the novel *Emila's Sentimental Journey*

．．．．．．．．．．．．．．．．．．The roly-poly Kazak girl was dressed elaborately in bright colors and wore a round showy hat to match. The Kazak boy was skimpily dressed and in my estimation wore only one layer of clothing. He had a monkey-like alertness and agility about him and seemed to enjoy talking down to us from his higher vantage point.

—From the novel *Valley of Eagles*

When my pupils finally adjusted to the light, I saw two women in the outer room, who were on their knees cutting carrots with Uygur knives shaped like scimitars. As I extended my greetings, they got on their feet to usher me in. "Come in, Lao Wang, come in please!" said the first woman. She was handsome and wore a white one-piece silk dress beneath which a light green petticoat vaguely showed through. The thick veins that stood out on her long neck and pronounced clavicle accented her thinness. Illuminated by the lightbulb, her oval face appeared ashen and worn, seemingly enveloped in sorrow. The butter-colored scarf thrown haphazardly about her head let strands of flaxen hair escape.

—From the novel *Pale Gray Eyes*

Two generations, two cultures,
two styles of attire: The past and
the future will always be with us.

—From recent writings

Granny started to build an earthen platform for a stove under the canopy of the tea stall. Building and repairing stoves was not only Granny's job but also seemed to be a great passion of hers. Every year she dismantled and built stoves, erected and swept chimneys. Every stove she built had neat, pleasing lines; all featured an ample superstructure supported on a substructure with a small footprint. Who knows but that the dimensions and proportions of those stoves might just unintentionally coincide with criteria of the beauty of Venus or Freudian psychoanalysis?

—From the novel *The Mud Hut with Its Door Left Ajar*

· · · · · · · · · · · · · · · · · The most striking thing about the house was its sparkling cleanliness. The spotlessness and shininess were reflected not only in the teapots, teacups, copper kettles, copper basins, windows, mirrors, and tables and chairs, the unpainted bare wooden window sills, exposed reed mats on the roof, and bare wooden rafters and the rug, neatly folded and arranged blankets, quilts and pillows on the *kang*, but also could be detected near the base of walls, doors and windows, and even on the mud floor (made of three fine coats of mud mixed with cow dung, I later learned).

—From the novel *Good Man Ismael*

Note: A *kang* is a heated brick bed widely used in northern China.

··············In front of their two-room house stood a lilac tree. When we arrived, its blooms had passed their prime, bringing to mind an aging beauty whose former glory was fading. Musa Ahun's two rooms were small but neatly kept. Their traditional-styled ceilings and floors were painted blue and red, respectively, and the windows with low sills opened on the street. The windows were protected on the outside by Russian-style wooden sashes with intricately carved patterns. Woolen rugs with floral patterns carpeted the interior floors of the house; the walls were decorated by a colorful Kuqa rug and a silk wall hanging of "Three Ponds of West Lake Mirroring the Moon."

—From the novel *Emila's Sentimental Journey*

· · · · · · · · · · · · · · · · Stalin Street ran to a residential neighborhood unlike others called Nuhaigur. It was laid out like a checkerboard, crisscrossed with neat, straight, and wide roads running north and south, east and west. They were all dirt roads that got dusty under the sun and muddy when it rained or snowed. I've never seen other houses like those in that neighborhood except in the illustrations to Chekhov's novels: raised porches accessed by wooden steps, four carved pillars supporting the gabled house and a carved wooden door that was normally kept closed, behind which stretched a dark hallway flanked by two rows of living quarters.

—From the novel *Leisurely Travels*

··················F or most households that didn't have a habit of reading books or news-
papers, kerosene lamps took no back seat to electric ones. The hardware store stocked all styles and sizes
of kerosene lamps. There were lamps for window wells, lamps to be put on desks, and lamps to be hung
on walls. "I need a size 10 kerosene lampshade." In Ili I learned to pick and buy these lampshades, which
broke easily and needed frequent replacements. The kerosene stored in big black steel drums in a corner
of Ili's hardware stores gave off a smell that actually evoked a sense of warmth and of hearth and home.

—From the novel *Leisurely Travels*

．．．．．．．．In the novel *Pale Gray Eyes*, I already celebrated the craftsmanship of Malk the carpenter. Cradles like this are works of art that embody a joyous blessing to the next generation. It is lined with layers of brightly colored home-spun sheets and quilts and at its side stands a *kang* table. The Uygurs' version of living in clover is "lying on twenty-four layers of quilts."

—From recent writings

NOTE: A kang is a heated brick bed widely used in northern China.

· · · · · · · · · · · · · · · · These three-and-a-half main rooms can be aptly described as high-grade. Their foundation is about 70 centimeters above ground level as well as above the grade level of other rooms. Four neatly aligned square pillars support the roof above their generous front porch. All their windows open toward the south and are close to the floor, because the Uygur custom of sitting on the rug when they conduct their daily business means a lower line of sight than that of the Han Chinese accustomed to sitting in chairs. With the windows facing the sunny south and closer to the floor, the rooms have better lighting. These windows, however, all open out toward the courtyard, in contrast to the custom of Ili residents who have their windows on the street side to facilitate their observation of the street scene. All the rooms have wood floors although the paint on them has peeled. Of special interest is their neatly planked ceiling whose dark yellow color gives it an antique aura. This coloration may have developed with the paint gone flat or the wood itself having oxidized with age.

—From the novel *Leisurely Travels*

· · · · · · · · · · · · · · · · · Ili is also famous for its smokeless coal (anthracite). According to an old comrade, whose whole family had moved lock, stock, and barrel from Henan Province to Xinjiang a long time ago during Sheng Shicai's tenure as Xinjiang Superintendent, the smokeless coal of Ili could be ignited with the strike of one match. During my eight years there, I did not have any such experience myself, although it is true that this coal ignites easily and possesses a superior ability to preserve itself. After the coal burns for some time, an ashy coat forms on its surface to sort of seal itself. A big chunk of coal thus "sealed" can be kept smoldering for several days; to restart a fire, one simply fishes from the ashes or borrows from a neighbor one such glowing nugget the size of an egg and in less than fifteen minutes a strong raging fire would be going.

—From the novel *Leisurely Travels*

· · · · · · · · · · · · · · · · · From then on this window took on a special meaning for us. The broken pane was eventually replaced. We later installed white curtains over it. We had the curtains made by a Uygur woman, whose embroidery skills transformed two ordinary pieces of white cloth into fascinating patterns of flowers and moons. It goes without saying that the patterns were genuinely Uygur.

—From the novel *Window on the Street*

Passing through three crudely made odd-sized wooden doors, one comes first to an earthen stove for making *nang* [crusty pancake]. This stove is called *nang keng* in the local dialect. At *nang* making time, black and white smoke billows up from the stove; next to the *nang keng* is the one and only glass window letting light into the squat mud house. This window does not open and what air circulates in the house filters in through the door cracks. The glass pane in the window is actually two sheets joined end to end; dust and greasy fumes have deposited a brownish yellow film on the window glass....

—From the novel
Mud Hut with Its Door Left Ajar

. . . . W̌e camped in a log cabin, not one of those
neatly assembled and nicely painted wooden huts, but a log cabin fit for a primitive savage. The four walls and the roof were all made with round logs shorn of
twigs and leaves but not of the skin and bark. They were joined and fastened
with big U-shaped nails (also known as centipede nails).

—From the novel *Valley of Eagles*

108

· · · · · · · · · · · · · · · · · · This vast grassy expanse is winter pastureland. It is not too cold even in winter because it is sheltered from the wintry gusts and receives ample sunlight. At this time, with all the cattle having migrated to the summer pastureland high up in the mountains, the grass on this winter grazing ground has entered a state of recuperation and has a chance to grow unmolested. The few wooden huts built in recent years as part of a settlement for herdsmen are deserted for now and appear quiet and forlorn. Due to the ample supply of timber and a shortage of construction workers in these mountains, most wooden houses seen in these parts have a particularly primitive air to them. People would cut down trees, saw them into desired lengths without bothering to skin them, arrange these logs (more properly called tree segments) next to one another and fasten them together with big "centipede" nails and a wall is born. After the erection of the four walls, a fifth built in the same manner is hoisted on top of them to serve as the roof, and a new house is completed.

—From the novel *Bedraggled Horse*

· · · · · · · · · · · · · · · · ·In October she had a well-attended wedding that was grand and fun-filled. Thirty some young people sang and danced in the festivity. Her hatmaker husband was as affectionate and solicitous toward her as before the wedding. She kept a neat and spotless house. You wouldn't be able to find a single speck of dust on the rugs with colorful ethnic designs. Toward the end of October, they installed a galvanized iron stove. The stove and its venting pipe were kept so polished they could double as mirrors.

—From the novel *Light of the Heart*

· · · · · · · · · · · · · · · · This is the most luxurious guesthouse in this small town. In the past only illustrious guests from Beijing or the capital of the Autonomous Region would be lodged here. Later foreign guests were also granted the privilege.

—From the novel *Light of the Heart*

· · · · · · · · · · · · · · · · · · · ·Muhamed Ahmed impatiently ushered me into the room. It was slightly better furnished, with a half new rug, a long table covered by a lacework tablecloth, displaying porcelain bowls of different sizes and a collection of hardcover tomes in old Uygur, which was very unusual. A wooden chest inlaid with yellow trim stood against the wall. A picture frame hung on the wall with, curiously, only photos of Ahmed, one showing him in a Russian student uniform with multiple buttons, looking very innocent and cute and another awkwardly re-colored and somewhat distorted picture of him wearing a suit. On another wall hung a square-bottomed basket for flour, a wooden basin for kneading flour, and two unfinished brooms made with millet stalks, as well as a huge pear-shaped object, which was a musical instrument called the dutar. I already made its acquaintance when I was in Turpan and South Xinjiang before I came to Ili.

—From the novel *O Muhamed Ahmed!*

· · · · · · · · · · · · · · · · · March came, finally! As snow started to thaw in late March, the streets and alleys turned into a mire. Under such circumstances even overshoes lost their usefulness in Ili and waist-high rubber boots were de rigueur. By April the mud became trickier, when waist-high rubber boots no longer protected one's trousers from being splattered with mud. The rubber boots sloshing in the mud did not make a squishy sound but rather a croaking sound like that made by frogs in midsummer in south China. This sound resulted from the bursting of a bubble formed by a transient vacuum, mixed with air and mud, and the subsequent filling of the vacuum by the watery mud.

—From the article "April Mud"

The traffic on the street consisted more often of trucks, Beijing jeeps, Soviet-made Gaz-69 jeeps, rubber-tired horse carts, four-wheeled horse carts, six-poled horse carts, two-wheeled donkey carts and large-wheeled ox carts. Sometimes Kazak herdsmen from the mountains, all bundled up in layers of clothing and equipment, could be seen riding on their horses in the street, unshaken in their belief that the asphalt was made for their iron-shod hooves, just as young people in their colorful ethnic dresses would march in the thoroughfare, singing arm in arm, oblivious to the possibility that this behavior could be in any way inconsistent with traffic regulations.

—From the novel *Light of the Heart*

· · · · · · · · · · · · · · · · · The biggest tree is found on Stalin Street. Its history probably goes back a long time. A common sight on the street is the luxurious four-wheeled, six-poled horse cart with its floor covered by a colorful floral-patterned rug. It is a Russian-style "tourist bus" with soft and fragrant hay underneath the rug and one end curled like the back of a park bench. Sometimes the cart drawn by three strong chestnut-colored Ili horses carries only a newlywed couple or an imam or a high official. The horse's neck is often adorned with red silk ribbons and copper bells. When the cart is in motion, the din of the four wooden wheels lined with sheet metal is accompanied by the ding-dong of the bells.

—From the novel *Leisurely Travels*

That is to say, in addition to the New Year's Day and the Chinese lunar New Year, the Muslims have two other holidays—also called "New Year": They are 'Id Rozah or Lesser Bairam (Festival of Fast-breaking) and 'Id al-Adha or 'Id al-Kurban (the Holiday of Sacrifice). The two holidays are forty days apart.

—From the novel *Splendors of a Frontier Town*

········ We have a Uygur saying that goes like this, "A giant gets so mad he loses his cool; a dwarf gets so mad he loses his life. The shorter one is, the shorter one's temper…."

—From the novel *The Mud Hut with Its Door Left Ajar*

· · · · · · · · · · · · · · · · Afarewell Nezir prayer meeting was organized before the departure. Those that came were mostly elderly people with long silvery beards, who were soberly dressed and knelt there unsmiling. I was deeply moved by the ceremony and the way they started to recite in unison the prayers asking for blessings on Daddy Mumin's safe travel and bon voyage in their unique lilting, sober, pious and aging voices, keeping in check an untamable passion.

—From the novel *The Mud Hut with Its Door Left Ajar*

· · · · · · · AUygur proverb says: "When one visits friends, one is accumulating credit for a return visit from them."

—From recent writings

"Tamashar" is a very common expression in Uygur. It means playing, strolling, gawking, and art appreciation; it can be used as a verb or as a noun. It is close to the English expression "to enjoy" but has a broader sense than that. When a Uygur uses the expression *tamashar*, there is always a relaxed sense of well-being in the speaker's tone and facial expression accompanied by a naughtiness.

—From the novel *Pale Gray Eyes*

· · · · · · · · · · · · · · · · The oases in the Ili river valley boast dense groves of white poplars, apple orchards on every farm, range lands on rolling hills and pastures in the highlands, timber forests and beekeepers who use their honey to brew moonshine *piwar* (i.e., beer) and Russian-style kvass. There is a Uygur tribe in Ili called the Taranchi, who are friendly and rugged in nature. Their greeting often consists of an amiable exchange of fisticuffs and the expletive: *"Anaun!"* [Something akin to "son of a gun"]

—From the novel *Leisurely Travels*

· · · · · · · · ·The young Uygurs are very generous and hospitable but set great store in reciprocating favors and good will. Someone who always takes but never gives, who enjoys being treated but never wants to treat others will not escape the sharp eyes of society and even sharper tongues and criticisms.

—From the novel *Splendors of a Frontier Town*

· · · · · · · · · Ｗhen I took a closer look, I was flabbergasted. His was such a small mattock! Even an underage girl's mattock is larger, not to mention regular mattocks used by men.

—From the novel *O Muhamed Ahmed!*

Following the example of Ismael, I also picked up a scythe and brought it down after mustering my strength…. Curiously I left a swath of stalks uneven in height that could not be bundled together because they formed an irregular, dispersed arc. Ismael paused to take out a small whetstone from his pocket. As he honed his scythe, he volunteered to instruct me in the art of scythe usage. He made me realize that I did not bend my back low enough, did not swing with an extended arm, that my scythe was too far from the ground and brought down at a less than ideal angle. More important, I should have brought the scythe down resolutely in one fell swoop. I acted on his instructions and after some practice was able to improve my performance markedly although I was still way behind the veteran farmer.

—From the novel *Good Man Ismael*

. . . . He perked up at the mention of his woodwork. He agreed that I was right: A grain of sand does not possess a soul but he and his woodwork do. He often had dreams of new designs of wooden chests, tables, chairs or cradles orbiting around him. Inspired by the novel ideas in the dreams, he would go straight from his dream to his workshop and, working furiously with adze, saw, chisel, and plane, put together a piece of wood furniture embodying a brand new design.

—From the novel *Pale Gray Eyes*

· · · · · · · · A̲s for headwear, I completely understand that the Uygurs must have their hats on, winter, spring, summer, and fall, indoors or outdoors. To doff one's hat in others' presence is very bad form.

—From the novel *O Muhamed Ahmed!*

· · · · · · · ·On the wall inside hung a large picture frame, showing presumably a photo taken from a painted portrait. The smashing man in the picture had a thick moustache above his upper lip and donned a hat fit for a Russian Cossack.... Needless to say, this was the husband of Svetkhan.

—From the novel *Leisurely Travels*

· After saluting the lady of the house, Cao Qianli ducked his head and walked into the yurt that preserved its colorful décor despite looking a bit rundown. The interior was sweltering, the fire under the silvery copper teakettle still smoldering. The floor in the room was covered from end to end by floral rugs; three elderly men sat around teacups arranged on a large tablecloth spread on the rug.

—From the novel *Bedraggled Horse*

········T he vehicle was driven at a breakneck speed, raising a maelstrom of sand dust in its wake. Sometimes the ride got so bumpy the passengers' heads hit the ceiling of the car. At a rest stop, they ate at a Uygur eatery offering baked stuffed buns. The service was very good.

—From the novel *The Last Tao*

· · · · · · · · · · · · · · · · · "In our ethnic tradition, when men dance, the movement of their upper arms is supposed to be kept beneath the level of the shoulders." He demonstrated a couple of the most common dance movements: "Only women raise their arms above their shoulders when they dance." He went on to demonstrate how women danced, to my great amusement. "But Muhamed Ahmed insists on dancing this way." He mimicked his "feminine" way of dancing.

—From the novel *O Muhamed Ahmed!*

· · · · · · · · · · · · · · · · The following is a joke circulating among the Uygurs: Our forefathers came to *Huda* [God] to seek a living. When a man from the mountains came to *Huda*, he was given an ax and ordered to make a living by cutting timber. When a man from the lakes sought help, he was given a net and instructed to fish for a living. A heavily built man who came to *Huda* was given a lance and the job of defending the country. Finally came two good-for-nothing freeloading bums, who came to blows in front of *Huda* as they vied for his favors. In his fury *Huda* picked up a chopstick and broke it in two, giving one piece to each and issued the imperial edict: "You will live out your life on beggars' sticks, dogging decent folks!"

—From the novel *Brigade Leader, Party Secretary, Wild Cat and Broken Chopstick*

141

王蒙和他的新疆

Mukam

Your passionate cry like erupting lava
Pierces the earth's crust thousands of years old.
Is it from joy or from the fury of life and death let loose?

You water thousands of miles of Gobi wild
With a pouring rain of affection.

Vermilion lips like ripe pomegranate
Implore the summer to stay.
Is it a dream craze, lost prayer bud, or seed?

You sweep away your heart's troubles,
Tangled threads of your melancholy
Unleashing the hurricane of language.

Your soft, lithesome figure swims
Like fish through fluffy white clouds,
An embrace, a shyness, a first date,
A tearful glance and 'tis time to part.

You breach the gate to a thousand rivers
The blind now see a star-studded sky.

It's singing voices, it's thunderclaps.
It's string and wind instruments,
Thousands of troops on steeds galloping.
It's dancing, it's bolts of lightning,
It's costumes and never-withered loving looks.
Every violent soul you tear up.
You dip in the spring of revival.

O lonely world and forlorn mountains,
Dunes of yellow sand with knotted brows.
Because of you the world of my Mukham
Is barren no more and mountains
No longer lonely and the vast desert,
Its forehead smoothed, wakes from agony.

O lonely men, sorrowful old folks,
Motherless children forgotten.
Thanks to you
The soul of Uygur Mukham is no longer lonely.
You can now grow old without fear.
Forgotten children have found their mother.
They will never lose her again.

What has sprung to life
As singing and music rise out of Mukham?
This is the world, this is humanity.
Youth, love, and pain give meaning to
Life and the living beings we are.

We are alive, we have all the world.
We will not forget life and the world
For we have Mukham, eternal Mukham,
Full of the living spirit of Mukham.

NOTE: Mukham, or "Twelve Great Melodies," is classic Uygur music
that has been part of their culture for many centuries.

                  · · · · · · · · · · · · · · · · · Of course I've heard about the famous Uygur singer Dilber. The two songs "When the Grapes are Ripe" and "My Beloved Shepherdess" interpreted by her became instant hits in China and have enjoyed popularity in Asia, Africa, and Latin America. When she sings, her body moves in a spontaneous way suggestive of Uygur folk dancing, her jade-white braceleted arms waving gently above her shoulders. It is always such a fascinating performance.

—From the novel *Valley of Eagles*

· · · · · · · · · · · · · · · · Who was the singer? The refreshing, earthshaking singing resonated with a deep, intimate, and nostalgic undertone. Of course this was not a melody of Kashgar folk origin nor was it a Kashgar way of singing. It could only come from my hometown, from the grass-carpeted Ili river valley, from its deep woods of white poplar trees. When the singing had finally stopped, I made my hesitant way toward the source of the singing voice to find out more. I was now able to see the singer, who sat in a corner of the square, his back humped, his dense black beard disheveled, and under his prominent forehead and bushy eyebrows, his deep-set eyes seeming wistfully to stare into the distance.

—From the novel *Song God*

· · · · · · · · · · · · · · · · The south Xinjiang folk songs, typified by "Anargul," possess a stronger rhythmic quality. When people sing these songs, they seem to be treading heavily, as if trekking on a stage route through the vast deserted Gobi of sand and gravel, with snow glistening on mountains in the distance and the dry kindling grass quivering in the wind. The wayfarers' singing is imbued with fortitude and affection. I seem to see on their faces the dark tan produced by the south Xinjiang sun.

—From the novel *Bedraggled Horse*

.... I never dreamed that I would once again, in my lifetime, in this desolate Gobi, under a blanket of white snow, get to hear the familiar and fascinating sound of Uygur songs. I stood transfixed by the door, forgetting I was looking for a seat.

Solo:
In bitter cold, snow, and ice, I yearn for spring.
When will the birds fly and the flowers be in full bloom?
When will the lasses beam with smiles?
When will we sing to our heart's content
and quench our thirsty hearts with ballads?

Chorus:
O spring, O spring,
We miss you! We yearn for you!

—From the novel *Song God*

. . . . Maybe these songs are meant to be sung on camelback. Riding on the "boats of the desert," they acquire an appreciation of the vastness, the desolation, the silent solitude, and mystery of Mother Earth, as well as their own leaping, burning, tortured, and resplendent inner flames. They have traveled many days and nights. They have searched for years. They have created many cities and villages. They thirst for more affection and love in the world.

—From the article "Songs of Xinjiang"

．．．．．．．．．．．．．．．．．． The vocalization technique was very unique, neither Italian, nor Chinese Han folk, nor Mongolian folk, nor any particular Xinjiang ethnic folk. The singing was characterized by a pronounced trembling as well as a mellifluous quality and a rich timbre. It was at once soft and serene as well as full-bodied and sober. I almost forgot he was an imam reciting from the Koran; rather I seemed to hear a folk singer interpreting a song about man, about life and death, about togetherness and separation, and about the universe and the infinite.

—From the novel *Leisurely Travels*

· · · · · · · · · · · · · · · ·In faraway Ili, nearly every native can sing "Eyes So Dark"; it is almost always sung when people meet for a drink. Medical theory about vocal cords may say singing and drinking do not mix; however, they both offer an emotional outlet, a chance at catharsis.

—From the article "Songs of Xinjiang"

The singing and the lute playing seemed to draw to an abrupt close. Then melancholy and mellifluous notes of a baritone wafted in the air, the quavering sentimentality sheathing a sword-like, chest-rending pain and a long pent-up, heavily oppressive angst. You felt lost, you lowered your head, and you became delusional. You seemed to see a long funeral procession, with mourners wearing white bands on their waists, crying: "Oh, my friend! Oh, my friend!"

—From the novel *Song God*

$\cdots\cdots\cdots I$ was levitated by the ascending melody; I soared and I flew over the vast homeland, land of freedom, the racing and roaring Ili River, the towering spruces on Tianshan Mountains, and the land carpeted by flowers in full bloom.

—From the novel *Song God*

Symphony II

The mud oozes tears.
Horses pull with all their might
To extricate their hooves from the mire.
The ground leans this way and that.
What a melancholy dance.
An elegant riddle
Veils the maiden's face.
Wheels move in ancient ruts.
Window after window opens
Sending up wispy curls of smoke.
Distant hills trail garlands,
Singing on the threshing ground
Night after night.

· · · · · · · · · · · · · · · · · The melancholy singing was now edged with a rising, wild, agitated cry, like a dark cyclone that suddenly struck the *Taklimakan* hinterland; the powerful imperial cyclone uprooted entire sand dunes, hoisted them into the sky, eclipsing the sun, and ruthlessly destroyed all fragile life. Weeds and wildflowers withered; fish, crustaceans, frogs, and other river life were buried under the river bed; topsoil was blown off, forming a column of dust rising into the sky; the parched earth cracked along wind-eroded grooves.

—From the novel *Song God*

·········Then he started to sing, celebrating youth, life, the ocean, the roaring wind,
the arm that wielded the blacksmith's hammer,
and the eyes of the lasses.

—From the novel *Bedraggled Horse*

· · · · · · · · Anargul means pomegranate flower and is a popular name for girls in south Xinjiang. It is a beautiful name. The title song of the movie *Anarkhan* was adapted from the folk song Anargul, which begins with:

How crisp my rawap sounds!
Has it been strung with golden strings?

—From the article *Songs of Xinjiang*

············· I fell in love with the folk songs of Ili. From my home in Yining City, I often heard people sing "Eyes So Dark" late in the night. I couldn't be sure whether it was sung by drunkards, homecoming travelers, or horse-cart drivers hurrying toward their destination. Their singing was laden with deep emotion, conveying in the cold, lonely night their love for the girl with dark eyes and their romantic fantasies. Life was harsh and sometimes sterile, but that did not stop them from singing with passion and tenderness.

—From the article "Songs of Xinjiang"

· · · · · · · · ·The songs of south Xinjiang with Kashgar as its center differ greatly from those of north Xinjiang, centered about Ili. If "Eyes So Dark" epitomizes north Xinjiang folk songs, then south Xinjiang folk songs are typified by Anargul.

—From the article "Songs of Xinjiang"

················H e took the decrepit *dombra* and played a tune on it. He had heard this tune titled "Early Spring" on two occasions before 1966; he didn't know why it suddenly came back to him. He started to play it from memory and improvised where memory blurred, startling the elderly lady and the three old herdsmen with his musical virtuosity.

—From the novel *Bedraggled Horse*

· · · · · · · · · · · · · · · · · ·I have never before heard songs that are at once so tender and yet so untamed as the folk songs of Kashgar. After hearing or singing these songs that are characterized by primitive tenderness and tender primitiveness, you feel you've given all your life, your body, and mind. I've never heard songs that are so melancholy, yet so serene and sweet as the folk songs of Ili. After hearing or singing them, you think you've experienced all the sadness, sweetness, bitterness, and pungency there is to experience in this world and have sublimated to a state where suffering and happiness are one and where there's no more worry about life or death.

—From the novel *Splendors of a Frontier Town*

"I love to *tansa!*" Humming a tune, he sprang to his feet and started to pace left and right, back and forth. My mood at that particular moment was totally incongruous with social dancing, and I did not even look his way. Sensing my lack of interest, he switched into a Uygur tune and a Uygur dance. Then he went panting to the wall and took down the *dutar*, a pear-shaped instrument. After strumming on it absent-mindedly for a while, he threw it aside and sighed, "My fingers have thickened from working with a mattock every day. How can I be expected to play the *dutar* now?"

—From the novel *O Muhamed Ahmed!*

NOTE: The word *tansa* is a derivative from the Russian word for dance.

· · · · · · · · · · · · · · · ·A bevy of colorfully dressed girls of different ethnicities greets my sight before I see the flowers in full, multicolored bloom. The girls of Ili love to stroll in groups; they walk with their arms slung over each other's shoulders, talking, laughing, and singing ever so affectionately and cheerfully. They sing in Uygur:

Da ge da mu yue li mang ai mi zi. [We march on the boulevard.]

—From the novel *Window on the Street*

· · · · · · · ·Out of the blue, a stentorian voice broke the continuity. Shifting his weight onto one arm and setting aside his lute, Akram threw his head back and started to sing to the first star that had ascended into the vast firmament. The booming voice was unique, almost out of this world; it evoked images of a deluge bursting the floodgates, spring blooms carpeting an entire hill in the space of one morning, a thousand elaborately dressed Uygur girls dancing, and clouds of golden wheat grains raining down on the threshing ground.

—From the novel *Song God*

王蒙和他的新疆

CHAPTER 5 | Animals and Affection

The roof of the small house was all crooked because the beam was irregular in shape. The chimney was built by the old landlady herself and coated with wattle and daub; it had the shape of a yam, tapering at the two ends and thick and round in the middle. The door was even funnier looking. It was composed of three pieces of wood planking of uneven thickness, loosely nailed together, and you could stick three fists through the crack between the upper edge of the door and the doorframe.

■ This crack became a passage for swallows. Not long after I moved in, I discovered two house swallows had built a nest on a rafter under the roof. During the day, they flew in and out, raising some dust from time to time, and making a plunk-plunk noise. At dusk the two swallows snuggling up to each other in their nest would sit motionless, but with their watchful eyes wide open, following my every move as I came home from work, lit the lamps, washed my feet, picked up a book and unmade my bed. I noticed that as their eyes followed my movements, their fluffy little necks also turned as I moved about. Their plumage was a shiny black, which turned into a violet sheen tinged with green in the last rays of the sun creeping through the crack above the door.

■ About a month later, four baby swallows were hatched; the featherless newborn swallows looked ugly and piteous. How vulnerable all newborn animals are! One baby swallow fell from the nest but did not die from the fall because the roof was quite low. I carefully picked up the poor still-breathing baby and put it back into the nest, but it was immediately thrown out by its parent. There was nothing I could do. The baby swallow died soon after birth.

■ A few days later, the remaining three babies who had survived started to peep. Countless times their parents flew out to search for food and came back flapping their wings. At the sight of their returning parents, the three hungry babies opened their beaks, seeming to cry, "Mom and Dad, I'm hungry. Feed me, feed me!" Their mouths were open so wide all I could see in the nest were the three pairs of pink trumpet-like jaws, three pointed beaks, and three bottomless maws. In that instant I was struck by the huge size of their mouths and the magnitude of their need as they waited to be fed. The pair of patient, loving, selfless and indefatigable adult swallows took turns feeding the worms they had caught into the babies' mouths. I once saw an adult swallow fly out to find more food after a baby swallowed a worm in a quarter of a second, and when another adult swallow flew back in, all the babies started to clamor, including the one who had just swallowed a worm. There was no modesty, no volunteering to wait, and no understanding of the virtue of taking turns on the part of the latter, who joined in the complaining, as if it had been starved for a week.

■ The racket of these babies clamoring to be fed, presumably at a high decibel, often woke me up in the morning or deprived me of the chance to take a noontime nap. But I did not resent them in the least; I found them to be lovely and felt close to them. This was a large family, consisting of a "couple" taking care of three "kids." The affection between the "wife and husband," the tender, loving care of the parents, and the innocent high spirits and cuteness of the kids added joys to life in my house. I had come to this unfamiliar place called the Maolayuzi Commune eight thousand li from home with only one suitcase with me and no ability to communicate in the local dialect. It was the eve of the Cultural Revolution, pregnant with ominous forebodings; the political atmosphere was dangerously charged, and arts and literature were in the dumps. As I, a man sent down here to be "tempered and reformed by labor," faced an uncertain future, this family of swallows helped make more tolerable the long hours of loneliness and solitude unique to that period.

Note: A li is a traditional measure of distance, approximately equivalent to one-third of a mile or half a kilometer.

One was a larger grayish white Plymouth Rock chicken, who turned its rigid neck and stared at another smaller noble-looking youngish rooster with golden red plumage. As they started to leap and jostle for a commanding height to pounce on the other, the children began to cheer. With the roosters locked in an inconclusive battle, two ducks swam over from the irrigation ditch as if they also wanted to be spectators.

—From the novel *Bedraggled Horse*

············· They were just being jealous of other animals
that were larger and had more stamina than they. That was why they were making all the blustering and menacing gestures. No horse, not even that inexperi-
enced and impulsive chestnut horse, would pay the least heed to them. The barking of these dogs might actually boost the ego of the riders, serving as it were a
herald of their arrival. All Uygurs, Kazaks, and Tartars were thus familiar with
one common saying, "Despite the dogs' barking, the camel caravan moves on."

—From the novel *Bedraggled Horse*

· · · · · · ·An old horse on its feet suddenly closes its eyes, and when it reopens the eyes, it will have taken a nap. That is a horse's sleep.

—From the novel *The Mud Hut with Its Door Left Ajar*

· · · · · · In south Xinjiang, people drink the silt- and sand-laden water from the main irrigation channel and share the room with the sheep. There's no better place than ours in the whole wide world!

—From the novel *Light of the Heart*

···············All one hears is the howling of winds: mountain wind, ocean wind, plateau wind, and high-altitude wind accompanied by the roaring of thousands of animals: tigers and lions, leopards and apes.... Once it breaks into a gallop, the horse stabilizes, and sitting on its back is like an armchair ride. All its problems are now gone and the only thing on its mind is running full speed ahead....

—From the novel *Bedraggled Horse*

· · · · · · · · · The apple trees were covered by snow-like blossoms; birds hopped about on the twigs and the canopy of the tea stall, and one could hear the loud lusty cries of cows, goats, donkeys, horses, dogs, cats, and chickens. In spring their calls were more passionate than in other seasons.

—From the novel *Emila's Sentimental Journey*

What quiet is there to speak of? You hear the crowing of the roosters, the barking of the dogs, and the rustling of the leaves. When you open the faucet, you hear the water gushing out. Then you hear the cars' engines revving and the horns blowing. Two days a week you also get to hear the buzzing of airplanes. Don't forget, too, human voices of all registers, multiethnic chitchat, and laughter. In spring you hear the warbling of all sorts of birds. Summer brings the hesitant croaking of toads. Crickets and click beetles join the symphony in autumn. Even windblown snowflakes in swinter make a swooshing sound, not to mention the crackling of burning firewood and charcoal.

—From the novel *Light of the Heart*

. . . . That's why everybody says it's safest to ride this old dapple-gray horse. Yes, when it has lost every other quality, it has gained the virtue of a safe ride. With safety comes everything; without safety, there's nothing. This is a true pearl of wisdom.

—From the novel *Bedraggled Horse*

· · · · · · · · · · · · · · · The singing electrified the old horse into a gallop. Its four hooves poised in the air, it ran like wind and lightning, like a whale cleaving through glittering ocean waves that parted and receded deferentially to make way for the conqueror, like a rocket cruising through the luminescent sky, with the assembled stars cheering and dancing. Beams of light of all colors, white, red, blue, green, and yellow, picked out a splendorous and phantasmagorical world.

—From the novel *Bedraggled Horse*

·········W arisjan asked me later, "Did you want to buy this bird to set it free? You would have wasted your time. The bird's owner is a friend of mine. He has domesticated this bird. He often takes it to the West Park and lets it out of the cage to fly for a while. At a whistle, the bird would come right back to the cage. What do you expect? He feeds yolk to the bird.

—From the novel *Leisurely Travels*

· · · · · · · · · · · · · · · ·All are back. All are back. You chestnut horse and roan horse, you lilac horse and white horse, are all back. You reins and halter, saddle and stirrups, neighing at the sky, sparks flying from the horseshoe striking the pavement, carefree shaking of the mane, and the warm and moist smell of horse sweat have all come back. Even the smell of horse sweat was refreshing. Without horse sweat, there would be no Halidam, or Uncle Izhaq, or Mr. Hajiz, or the Kazak way of life. Your Kazak girl who leaps onto her horse without the aid of stirrups or a grip on the mane has come back!

—From the novel *The Last Tao*

·········"Sigh, my friend! My pal! Is there another horse like you? You are cowardly like a mouse, insignificant like an ant, and unresponsive like a clay figurine or wood sculpture," muttered Cao Qianli. He mumbled some more words to the horse before finally heaving onto the horse. Horses are destined to be ridden by people; there's nothing you can do about it. The horse indifferently started to trot at a leisurely pace. Cao Qianli was so full of compassion, pity, and love for the horse that every lifting of a hoof, every quiver of an equine ear, every ripple of a vertebra, every twist of the horse's rump, every twitch of its belly, every flaring of its big nostrils, and every snort would elicit a corresponding movement in Cao Qianli's own four limbs, his ears, his spine, his backside, his belly, and his nostrils. His every organ and every muscle would experience the same strain, the same tension, the same excitement, the same fatigue, and the same pain as the horse. Maybe it was not he who was riding the horse but the horse that was riding him. Maybe the animal whose four hooves moved with difficulty on the arid sand and hot gravel and who was weighed down with cargo was Cao Qianli himself.

—From the novel *Bedraggled Horse*

· · · · · · · · · · · · · · · · The black and white cat was given to me by an old watchman tending a melon patch in the village and his chain-smoking young wife. As we moved from my old place on Liberation Road to this small compound, we brought the cat along. Whenever we contemplated a short stay at the Maolayuzi Commune, we would take it to Daddy Mumin's mud house with its door always left ajar. The cat was at first confused by the change of environment but soon got used to it. After a few times, the back and forth relocations became an acceptable routine for the cat. Once out of its transport (a tote bag), it was able to quickly familiarize itself with the new environment and began to climb walls and trees without any inhibition. It was especially good at recognizing my voice. In the city or the countryside, whenever it heard the clanking of the mud guards on my bicycle, which was in slightly better shape than Warisjan's, it would run the dozens of meters to meet me, meowing affectionately and rubbing its cute little face against my leg. This must be a cat's way of kissing.

—From the novel *Leisurely Travels*

· · · · · · · · · The warbling of a lone bird soon transported me away from the workaday world. It sounded like a gurgling brook, a bagpipe, a string instrument, a song, as if pouring out its heart, its admiration, or laughing. This was indeed a song from heaven, a song from the forest, a song from the mountains.

—From the novel *Leisurely Travels*

The Kazaks are a rugged, hardworking people. The romanticized and mythologized version of Kazak life exists only on the silver screen. They herd their sheep and cattle from place to place regardless of seasons, sunshine, rain, winds, or snow. At yeaning or shearing times or when wolves and bears start to roam, they guard their livestock day and night. They have no Sundays, no New Year's Day, no Spring Festival; even on the Festival of Fast Breaking and 'Id al-Kurban, they cannot afford to enjoy total rest. They ask so little of life: an annual sojourn for two months, in July and August, on the summer pastureland, the vast space high up in the mountains, the aroma of horse milk, the fattened lambs. That is enough for them; that's a sufficient reward for their yearlong labor.

—From the novel *The Last Tao*

Daddy Mumin kept a strongly built albeit smallish female donkey for transport. Having foaled just over a month ago, it had not been ridden by Daddy Mumin for quite a while. This evening he really needed the donkey, but the latter was reluctant to leave its foal behind and kept making circles about Daddy Mumin, who held the bridle in a tight grip. With its mouth forced wide open by the tightened reins, the exposed pink gum and tongue and the flared nostrils made for an ugly sight. Despite the yelling of Daddy Mumin, whose face became flushed with straining, the donkey simply wouldn't budge. Even the shrill reprimands of the old mistress failed to produce any effect. The elderly couple and the donkey were locked in a tug of war whose outcome was a toss-up.

—From the novel *The Mud Hut with Its Door Left Ajar*

王蒙和他的新疆

| Heavenly Food and Divine Beverages

After preparing some vegetables and dough balls, Auntie put a big iron pot's worth of water on the stove. As the water started to boil, she moved some red-hot firewood away to one side and went out of the little courtyard to stand in the middle of the road. She watched for a while before coming back in. Lifting up the big wooden lid from the pot, she saw that a quarter of the water had evaporated. She added some water with a dipper gourd and rekindled the firewood, which had been temporarily moved aside to bring the water to a boil again. Then she reduced the fire and went out to wait. The same routine repeated several times still produced no sign of the old man but rather a waste of water and firewood. I hurried out with the shoulder pole and pails to draw more water. The old lady's two tinplate pails came in unmatched sizes and the pole was hand-made from a tree branch and retained its round cross-section. At one end of the pole was a hook with two rings made by a blacksmith; at the other was a homemade hook of thick galvanized wire bent into shape with a pair of pliers. As one carried the empty pails on the pole, the latter kept rolling on one's shoulder and the pails swung about making a racket. Luckily these pails were much smaller and lighter and held less water than the cast-iron cylindrical ones used in farming communities south of the Great Wall. Besides giving the shoulder a bad time, carrying these pails of water was not a particularly backbreaking job. When I came back with the water, the old lady of the house was still engaged in the Sisyphean labor of adding water and firewood, cooling and re-boiling the water. I couldn't help offering the advice: "Why don't you start boiling the water when the old man arrives? You've boiled the water several times over and there's still no sign of him. Maybe he's not coming back today."

■ Her favorite pastime was drinking tea, the *fuling* tea (tuckahoe, poria coccos) from Hunan. She prepared it like a traditional Chinese herbal medicine. By May 1966, I'd stayed nearly a year in their home; one afternoon we sat under the thick foliage of the apple tree to take milk tea; the sunlight filtered through the branches swaying in the breeze threw a dappled shade on the ground. The dried *nang* [crusty pancake] dipped into the tea constituted a meal. After several days of practice, I was already able to down two big bowls of milk tea at a time (each bowl could hold about 1.5 kilos of water). This was a feat for a non-local like me. After drinking 3 kilos of milk tea and eating a corresponding amount of *nang*, I felt content but fatigued. I went back to my small mud hut no larger than 4 square meters and lay down to take a nap on the rug I had bought for 11 *yuan* in the Street of the Hans in Yining City. After napping for 45 minutes, I got up to go to work. Before leaving the house, I saw Ayimhan still drinking milk tea, now with her neighbor Kuwahan opposite her, under the apple tree. Kuwahan, who was two or three years younger than Ayimhan, was married to a blacksmith. The two women liked to swap stories and gifts; whenever some delicious food was prepared by one, the other was sure to get a taste of it. The fact that Kuwahan's arrival had escaped my notice confirmed that I had dozed off for that time.

· · · · · · ·At this juncture,
he started to hum a tune with
the following lyric:

Who is better?
Mimi or Gigi?
Whomever you pick.
Which is plumper?
Water or sweet melon?
Whichever you eat.

—From the novel *Good Man Ismael*

. . . . H e invited me to a formal dinner where he served *dabanjin* [hand-pulled noodles], a local favorite in Ili. He made the dough himself. His way of making hand-pulled noodles (also called *lamian* or *lahman* in local parlance) was a departure from the local custom, which consisted of first breaking the dough into small sections that were then pulled into thin strands one by one and hung like skeins of wool over the table's edge to be boiled a skein at a time. He, on the other hand, knelt on the floor and kneaded a large amount of dough, which he greased with cooking oil and piled into a huge mound in the shape of coiled incense. When the water in the pot came to a boil, he started to pull the dough at a fast pace into long strands, which he fed into the pot without interruption until it was full, whereupon he severed the strands from the dough.

—From the novel *O Muhamed Ahmed!*

．．．．．．．．．．．．．．．．．I forced myself to eat a large bowl of beef entrails boiled in water seasoned with only a pinch of salt. When the old lady offered another bowl of soup laced with melted butter, I declined. She was greatly puzzled by my refusal of a hearty entrails soup laced with grease at a time when the scarcity of meat and oil was becoming more and more acute.

—From the novel *Mud Hut with Its Door Left Ajar*

. . . . As the old lady prepared the tea, she fed some bare corncobs into the recently installed rickety galvanized iron stove to start a fire. The small mud hut immediately became very warm and the old lady's face was flushed in the glow of the stove fire. With the fire dying down, the room noticeably cooled down again.

—From the novel *Mud Hut with Its Door Left Ajar*

· · · · · · · · · · · · · · · · · The fourth round of toasts started, of course, with the "wine magistrate," which happened to be your humble servant, myself. Pouring myself a bowl of wine, I knelt down holding the bowl and said, "I propose to recite a poem and dedicate this toast to Turdi. I invite him to also recite a poem or sing a song before drinking it." Turdi's eyes instantly lit up; he looked a little puzzled but was very much intrigued. I cleared my throat and started:

Read more pleasurable books
When you have free moments.
Don't let grass of melancholy
Take root in your sentiments.

—From the novel *Valley of Eagles*

· · · · · · · · · · · · · · · · ·I was extremely pleased by this special favor and privilege. Moreover, I became more of an oenophile during those years of upheavals and my close association with ethnic minorities and farm labor. The wine I liked was not just any wine but the "hooch" I saw the old man brew. It aged through all the four seasons of the Ili River Valley. I poured a little of this hooch in a small wooden spoon and as I gingerly tasted it with the tip of my tongue, I nearly let out a loud cry: "This is not alcohol! This is vinegar! No, it is not vinegar either, it is hydrochloric acid!" Indeed it was so caustic my tongue felt as if it were on fire.

—From the novel *The Genie of Grapes*

Twin-String Exercise

The sour and acerbic brew reflected the sparkling
   translucence of grapes.
The sweet grapes may not envy the tartness and
   bitterness of the fermented juice.

· · · · · · · · · · · · · · · · ·As late autumn rain gave way to early winter snow, cuttings had been taken from the grapevine and buried and the vines were pruned back. After the sun came out, I looked at the snow-capped Tianshan Mountains through the prism of the lonely bottle containing the fermenting grape juice and saw a mysterious, distorted world. When the winds were calm, the early winter sun still provided some warmth. Inside the mottled glass wall of the bottle, I found the calmed grape juice returning to activity and starting to churn and bubble. The bottle contained, in my imagination, not the grape juice to be brewed into wine but the genie of the *Tales of a Thousand Nights*.

—From the novel *Genie of the Grapes*

· · · · · · · · · · · · · · · · · · Warisjan offered to help and, digging with his mattock, created a makeshift stove. With a large bottle of vegetable seed oil, an ample supply of mutton, carrots, and bags of rice, he made enough *polo* [Uygur pilaf] for fifty people. I couldn't for the life of me figure out how and where they had gotten hold of all those rare commodities.

—From the novel *Leisurely Travels*

Take for example the drinking of milk. City people are accustomed to milk bottled in standardized glass containers. On Liberation Road or Stalin Street in Ili, milk is sold from carts dispatched by the rural production brigade of the Chabuchar milk farm. The galvanized iron tanks containing the milk are loaded on donkey carts and the milk purveyors use half-kilo or one-kilo dippers to dispense the milk, much in the way soy sauce and vinegar are dispensed to customers in state-run grocery stores.

South of the "city walls," milk is sold by youngsters from the ethnic communities. This milk has been precooked for a long time because the locals buy milk mainly to make milk tea. The precooked milk comes with milk skin floating on its surface, which makes for tastier milk tea than that prepared with fresh milk.

—From the novel *Leisurely Travels*

"Come here, come over to the table and have some tea!" The ladies offered their warm hospitality to me. I had intended to have some plain water instead of the salty and greasy milk tea but upon their insistent urgings I took a bowl of the offered brew. The hot beverage brought out a soaking sweat and freshened me up. I was persuaded that drinking brick tea and milk tea under the trees in mid-spring was indeed a great enjoyment in the life of the farm folks of the ethnic communities in border areas.

—From the novel *Mud Hut with Its Door Left Ajar*

. . . . After rounds of tea were served and loaves of *nang* [crusty pancake] consumed, I was reminded of an apt Uygur saying: "Great wealth tempts one to squander one's money; much *nang* eaten leads to much tea drinking." Indeed there is this virtuous cycle between *nang* and tea: the more *nang* you eat, the more you thirst for tea and the more milk tea you drink, the more you hanker for more *nang*.

—From the novel *Pale Gray Eyes*

⋅ ⋅ ⋅ ⋅ ⋅ ⋅ ⋅ ⋅ ⋅ ⋅ ⋅ ⋅ ⋅ ⋅ ⋅ ⋅ ⋅ In spring they were still threshing wheat harvested the previous year. This would be unheard of south of the Great Wall. In the aftermath of persistent autumn rains, much of the wheat started to germinate. This winter all the flour sold on the market in Ili, including Yining City, was milled from this kind of sticky wheat. Buns made from it tended to stick to the teeth even after having been steamed for over two hours.

—From the novel *Mud Hut with Its Door Left Ajar*

The youngsters selling milk carried small clay pots resembling the "cricket pots" of Beijing kids. On the hook dangling from either end of the shoulder pole hung, not the traditional single "main line," but multiple radiating lines of pots of evenly distributed milk and boiled milk skin at a *jiao* [Chinese dime] a pot. The pots all came with a small mouth and a "potbelly" designed to minimize spills. Every morning and late afternoon, droves of these kids combed the streets and alleys hawking their milk. They actually hawked not their milk but: "Milk skin, milk skin!" The shrewd house-wives would then come out from their homes and inspect closely the skin in each pot to pick the best quality and thickness. Sometimes several milk boys carrying their clinking pots of milk would show up in our yard at the same time, competing for business by deploying their respective skills of eloquence but never getting into a fight. The lucky kid who got his dime's worth of business transacted would imp-ishly and apologetically make a grimace toward the less lucky competitors in a show of the generosity that typically came with triumph.

—From the novel *Leisurely Travels*

$\mathbb{A}$mong all the stews, the most delicious is *mian fei zi*. After the dough is made, it is washed to produce starchy water and gluten. The liquid starch is pumped into cow lungs, inflating them to 5 times (Gasp!) the size of the lungs of the old cow when it took a deep breath. The lungs are then sealed and stewed together with its liver, tripe, kidneys, and intestines. The finished stew has the smell of chopped, cooked entrails of oxen and the smooth, chewy consistency of buckwheat pudding (cut into strips and served cold), which is a summer favorite of northerners. The beef is then cured for future consumption.

—From the novel *Pale Gray Eyes*

· · · · · · · · · · · · · · · · · The canopy of the tea kiosk might be crude but its installation enabled us to drink tea, have meals, and chat day or night outdoors. From March when the first snows had only thawed partially till late October when sleet began to form, we spent most of our time outdoors. In summer we stayed out and were loath to turn in until very late in the night. Despite the smallness of the yard, of the orchard, and of the door that couldn't shut properly, there was so much warmth and life about us. Even the small sparrows enjoyed sitting on the twigs above the canopy and sometimes decided to land on the ground a few feet from the humans sitting cross-legged and drinking tea. They also chitchatted as they hopped about. The swallows, always in pairs, were often seen flying about the tea kiosk making affectionate small talk.

—From the novel *Mud Hut with Its Door Left Ajar*

· · · · · · · · · · · · · · · · The *zhua fan* [pilaf eaten with hands] sent up appetizing aromas, and especially alluring were the pieces of mutton sitting on the rice bathed in oil and slices of carrots. This was a choice delicacy whose sublime colors, aromas, appearance, and taste were undreamed-of for people living south of the Great Wall. The four elderly men immediately went to task: with their index, middle, third fingers, and the pinkie formed into a spoon shape to scoop up the rice and the thumb in charge of tamping it down, they sent the morsels to their mouths and sometimes licked their fingers to mop up the kernels of rice and oil stuck on them.

—From the novel *Leisurely Travels*

· · · · · · · · · · · · · · · This stay had the feel of a long, leisurely, and languorous montage. We enjoyed seven-and-a-half hours of total relaxation and contentment, an unusual blessing in the climate of those times and given the plight I was in. Maybe only in times and circumstances such as those was it possible for me to come to terms with that striking simplicity, that unworldly tranquility, that unperturbed peace that seemed to turn people back into children in all their innocence. Everything was down to the plainest level: sipping tuckahoe tea, eating sunflower seeds baked to a perfect crispness, talking about the weather, mutton, grapes with family, half sitting, half lying on the quilt, stuffing a pillow under your small back, cutting meat and vegetables and kneading dough unhurriedly in your presence. There was probably nothing "deluxe," nothing "VIP," nothing luxurious about the stay. But everything went on in the happiest mood and with all sincerity and seriousness.

—From the novel *Emila's Sentimental Journey*

W hen it's time to harvest the ripe grapes in autumn, you have to fight off the birds that come to reap the sweet fruits. There is also a species of wild bees that sap the grapes of their sweet juice through the skin of the fruit, causing them to shrivel. These shriveled grapes are still edible. I rather like their taste because what little juice is left by the bees seems to have a sweeter taste.

—From the novel *Mud Hut with Its Door Left Ajar*

The fruits on the trees growing in farmers' gardens are yours for the picking. The Uygurs and Kazaks believe that whatever is spent for their guests' enjoyment will bring double rewards from *Huda* [God]. If guests take a hundred apples from your tree, then this tree will bear an extra two hundred apples next year, or maybe even a thousand bigger, sweeter, and tastier apples. If a guest receives a bowl of milk from you, then your milk cow may produce five extra pails of milk tomorrow. What a beautiful belief!

—From the novel *Mud Hut with Its Door Left Ajar*

················After we came back from the day's labor, the old lady announced that she was not preparing a meal because she had not been able to buy any meat. According to the Uygur custom in Ili, a meal consists of noodles, pilaf, wontons, dumplings, or pasta soup. Eating *nang* [crusty pancake] and drinking tea may assuage hunger but in no way constitutes a meal. This night we had to be content with *nang* and tea again. I had thought that after non-stop drinking at noontime and all afternoon, Auntie Ayimhan wouldn't be able to imbibe anymore, but to everyone's surprise she drank another two bowls.

—From the novel *Mud Hut with Its Door Left Ajar*

. . . . Unwrapping the bundle, he took out some neatly cut pieces of newspaper. He folded one sheet, making a crease, and pinched with two fingers a small amount of slightly above-average *Mohe* tobacco, by the looks and color of it, deftly distributing it evenly on the paper, licking an edge of the paper and rolling it into a cigarette. Then he lit it up, took a pull on it and passed it to me first, in deference to my age (I was the oldest of the three). He handed the young militiaman a small sheet and a pinch of tobacco, then made himself another one, took two pulls on it and resumed his account.

—From the novel *Pale Gray Eyes*

王
蒙
和
他
的
新
疆

Then I lay down. In the darkness, I kept smiling at the blue star peeking through the cracks in the wooden roof. The blue star later disappeared and snowflakes started falling through the cracks. Thanks to the white yam liquor and the smoldering embers, the snowflakes did not feel cold but rather fresh and gentle. I didn't even wipe them off my face. How wonderful that it was snowing lightly indoors as well!

■ I remembered a stanza of my favorite poem, *Rubaiyat,* by Omar Khayyam, which I had recited moments ago:

Ah, make the most of what we yet may spend,
Before we too into the dust descend;
Dust into dust, and under dust, to lie,
Sans wine, sans song, sans singer, and—sans end!

■ It inspired me to compose a five-character Chinese classical poem:

wu shi xu xun huan. [Enjoy while you can when everything's fine.]
you sheng mo duan chang. [You are alive, there's no reason for grief.]
qian huai shu gong jiu, [Amuse yourself with books and wine,]
he wen shou yu shang. [Whether your life is long or brief.]

■ A night of snow painted the country white.

■ Every blade of grass and every grain of sand bore the weight of the snow and received its caress. Every single twig, every single evergreen needle, and even the erect tree trunks were touched by the snow, which was present without discrimination on all parts of everything under heaven in greater or lesser amounts and for longer or shorter stays.

■ The snow snuggled up to everything. Our wooden house was nearly buried under it and started to look like a snow bank or snow dune. When the earth beckoned lovingly, snow would from time to time slip down from the trees, the grass, or the roof to kiss this vast land.

■ Snow laid a soft white carpet on the earth and imparted new splendors to the swaying dragon spruce trees. The white snow on the dark brown tree trunks, covered with vertical gouges, and on the dark green conifer needles seemed like glitters that emanated from the spruce trees themselves and accented them in a chiaroscuro contrast. Against this white backdrop, the goshawks spread their mysterious and stately wings.

■ In the white valley, steam rose from the water in the creeks whose color was a heightened blue, like that of the rain-washed sky bathed in sunlight. The rocks donning the pure white caps looked jaunty and sprightly.

■ The sun came out. The world was aglitter. Let's cheer this constantly renewing and ever bright world! People are the hope and fruit of the world. In response to your loud and drawn-out cheers, flakes of snow started to fall softly from the tops of the towering spruce trees.

■ How many El Dorados, how many serendipitous discoveries are there in the world? How zestful is life that tastes like aged wine? When snow buried a wooden cabin deep in the mountains up to its roof, when snow blocked the entrance to the doorless log cabin, when the Kazak truck driver carted away the roe deer meat he had sought, when the shepherd's children lit a golden bonfire with the twigs they hewed from high branches of the spruce trees, when the work songs of Shandong folks echoed through the frontier mountains, when our colleagues celebrated in their respective homes the twenty-second national birthday, when white yam wine warmed one's heart and chest, Turdi remembered the beautiful girl from Artux who betrayed his love. And the recitation of a poem by an eleventh century Persian scholar famous for his Jalali calendar broke the quiet of a lonely mountain night and triggered wonderful reverberations in one's heart.

······Culture created stone grottoes, sculptures, and mural paintings; nature nurtured the growth and continuation of culture. Our forefathers have left their mark and example that will last for millennia and our contemporaries recognize how much they owe to their ancestors.

—From recent writings

· · · · · · · · Lulled by the light of the blue star creeping in the log cabin, I fell fast asleep and started to dream, completely oblivious to my physical existence or where I was. I had a vague sense of walking again in the alley of my childhood Beiping (now called Beijing); the small alley seemed such a long passage to the child that I was and every step felt like treading on clouds.

—From the novel *Valley of Eagles*

Flute Concerto

Was last year's snow heavier or lighter?
Heavy snow, light snow, endless snow,
Softly falling flakes whirl and flutter,
Red burning tree sap set aglow
Flowed out of dirty eye corners,
Souring cucumbers and honey
After so many snow showers.
My wife's still not home from her journey.

Kanas Lake II

How pristine is Lake Kanas unspoilt
Alone amid tall peaks so picturesque.
The crowds carouse in high spirits.
I withdraw in quiet solitude.
Tides may follow the moon's wax and wane,
I'm in no mood to swim with the tide.
The lake pours straight into the Arctic,
Endless dirty tricks to wash away.

· · · · · · · From under the hard and arid earth's surface, sweet and fresh water is drawn from the qunat (*karez*) system of underground wells. Painstaking and skillful labor has produced a tourist attraction that is uniquely Uygur.

—From recent writings

Birds

Can you imagine a world absent
The wings of birds and fearless flying
Or a day when the sky falls silent?
Life would become so unedifying.

·······Farm irrigation in Xinjiang works in a way that is completely different from that practiced south of the Great Wall. Here irrigation is done in broad strokes, with voluminous water flowing in big channels that flood entire fields whose area ranges anywhere from five to twenty *mu* and that do not need to be subdivided into smaller plots enclosed by ridges for irrigation purposes.

—From the novel *The Mud Hut with Its Door Left Ajar*

NOTE: One *mu* is approximately 666.7 square meters.

Τhis place was originally called Aktil (white thorn grass). A hundred years ago, this was a vast wasteland overgrown with white thorn grass. Three poor men in pursuit of a roe deer stumbled upon this place where they discovered a parcel of land once inundated by flash floods from the mountains. The three of them collected wheat seeds in their inverted *dopas* and broadcast the golden kernels on this newfound land. Soon the wasteland began to yield food crops. I often think if three poor men were able to reclaim this land and settle down here a hundred years ago, then we the lucky successors and masters of the new society have no reason not to triumph over the sandstorms and reclaim more land on which to achieve unprecedented high yields.

—From the novel *Brigade Leader, Party Secretary, Wild Cat and Broken Chopstick*

NOTE: A *dopa* is a colorfully embroidered cap worn by Uygurs.

. . . . Only after I had lain down did I find that except for the floor, all the remaining five sides of this log cabin were leaky. I could clearly see stars and the sky through the cracks in the roof. After taking off my glasses, I had a strong impression, either because of my astigmatism or my myopia, that a star had entered the cabin through the cracks to become a lambent light hanging inside our little house. With the fluttering of my eyelashes, the "lamp" bobbed up and down, swelled or shrank in size. It looked at first like a lotus root and then like an eggplant, but it always retained its brightness. "Go to sleep, deep in the mountains," the star seemed to say to me.

—From the novel *Valley of Eagles*

· · · · · · · ·As the dogs stopped barking, the cows stopped mooing, the water in the mountain creek fell silent, the wind died down, the snoring of the old man subsided, and the cacophony of all those singers, domestic and foreign, vanished into thin air. All that was left was a world of moonlight, of silence, and early morning frost quietly and surreptitiously descending on the small yurt.

—From the novel *The Last Tao*

$\cdots\cdots\cdots\cdots\cdots\cdots$I had another unforgettable experience in 1972, when several comrades of the "May 7" Cadres' School were mobilized to load timber onto trucks in the Que Er Gou logging area of Hutubi. We were told that beyond the mountain ahead lay the Xinyuan County of Ili. As we surveyed the massive mountain, I jokingly suggested that we should just climb up that mountain and tumble down its side with our eyes closed until we landed in Ili. At this, a cheer went up from some comrades of non-Han extraction.

—From the novel *Leisurely Travels*

· · · · · · · · · · · · · · · · The darkness in the small log cabin in the mountain gully gave way to the warmth and beauty brought to life by the flicker of golden flame. The fluttering, quivering flame seemed like a mysterious signal, speaking a language as ancient as the sky and the earth and as indecipherable. The blue, yellow, white, and red tongues of the flame danced, changing partners; blue, white, and black whiffs of smoke rose and dispersed, their molecules in the millions assailing our faces, making them itch with the intense heat. We were intoxicated by an indescribable elation, stronger yet perhaps than that of acing the national magistrates' exam or of ascending to the throne.

—From the novel *Valley of Eagles*

·······All this is at once so novel and so familiar. Why do I not in the least feel ill at ease? I've never set foot on this mountain but everything here feels so close to me as if we had known each other for a long time and had made a date and expected this encounter. As if we had been in search of each other in our previous incarnations and had at long last found and met each other!

—From the novel *Valley of Eagles*

· · · · · · · · · The Grand Mosque of Kashgar appeared on the screen. As Guldam, the child, was sold by a human trafficker and the cruel bey trampled on the bouquet of red flowers given Guldam by Amil, we heard a grief-laden voice singing:

Why have the flowers wilted?
Why are they withered?

—From the novel *Splendors of a Frontier Town*

Stone Forest

Is it brimming talent
Enlightened temperament
The strain of disequilibrium
Or sedimentation of experience
That has created these towers?
This mystical forest of stone…
The Earth imagines the shapes,
We spin the yarns,
Mocking the rigid horizon.

．．．．．．．．．．．．．．．．．There are poplars and only poplars in Ili. Cathay poplars, white poplars, Xinjiang poplars, and Canadian poplars. A graduate of the Suzhou Medical School who was sent down to Ili decided one day to see the parks of Ili shortly after his arrival. In his experience, the surest way of finding a park in a small town was to look around for dense clumps of trees. But that did not work in Ili. In Ili trees are everywhere.

—From the novel *Leisurely Travels*

· · · · · · · ·As for me, I made only three cradles. Labor transformed the apes into humans. My labor has produced three cradles. Brothers, how do you like them? Look at this round ornament! Look at the curved carvings! The colors! No, these are not cradles; they are nuggets of gold, they are jewels, they are happiness. Children who sleep in these cradles will grow up to be worthy successors.

—From the novel *Pale Gray Eyes*

It is only natural that Wang Meng should write fascinating accounts of Xinjiang. Wang Meng went to Xinjiang in his prime (when he was 29) and spent 16 years of his life there. He gave his best to Xinjiang.

■ Wang Meng's odyssey took him to Urumqi, where he lived for a period. His footsteps also covered such areas as the oases of Ili, where he labored with Uygur mattocks, the Pamirs 16,405 ft. (5000 m) above sea level, the vast Bosten Lake, the Tianshan and the Kunlun mountains, and the banks of the Irtysh River, the Ili River, the Yarkant River, and the Tarim River. Wang Meng lived and toiled with people from different ethnic backgrounds and shared their joys and sorrows. Remembrances of his days in Xinjiang never fail to bring him joy, pride, and contentment as well as profound stirrings of emotion. He is intimately acquainted with every minute detail of that land, and his attachment to its people, its places, and the friendships he formed is deeply imprinted in his soul.

■ It is no small wonder that the sight of Wang Meng bursting into tears in the arms of his Uygur friends on his return to Xinjiang moved the bystanders to marvel: "What a moving scene! Such a nice man is hard to come by!" It is no wonder that when she overheard Wang Meng read aloud in Uygur, his Uygur landlady, who had not seen who the reader was, asked: "What radio station is broadcasting this program?" And it is no wonder that Uygur folks coming to town to visit Wang Meng would often hesitate at his door, unsure whether it was indeed his home, because its windows were decorated with uniquely Uygur lace curtains with intricate designs.

■ Wang Meng mastered Uygur not long after his arrival in Xinjiang. This enabled him to integrate seamlessly into its multiethnic society, like a fish swimming in its natural habitat—the ocean of life. He observed, experienced, and explored life from the perspective of a novelist and found the people, the land, and the sky there to be special and unique. His novels, prose writings, and poems with Xinjiang motifs exude life. Under his pen, Xinjiang leaps to life and reveals its charms. This collection presents a brand new vista, grand and yet intimate, stately and colorful. The photos by Arkin Khadir, a Uygur photographer, and others transport readers to that beautiful, exotic land. This is indeed a classic, intriguing, and memorable work!

—Fang Rui
Spring 2004